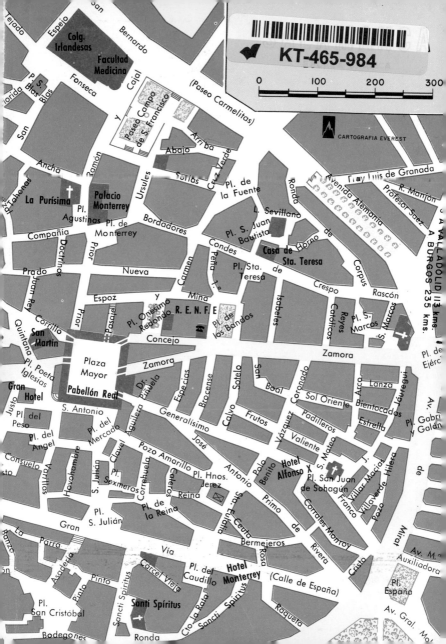

SALAMANCA

Texto: JULIÁN ALVAREZ VILLAR

Photographies: Oronoz

EDITORIAL EVEREST, S. A.

MADRID • LEON • SEVILLA • GRANADA
VALENCIA • ZARAGOZA • BARCELONA • BILBAO
LAS PALMAS DE GRAN CANARIA • LA CORUÑA

...constitute the city's coat of arms and together with the clubs of Count Raimondo sum up the history of Salamanca.

A ford across the Tormes, opposite a high embankment on the right of the river which was easily defendible, was the point at which a nucleus of primitive inhabitants first settled; this has been confirmed by prehistoric findings. They were followed by some settlers of Celtic origin who have bequeathed to us The Bull of The Brigde, a symbol of the city at all times, metioned in Lazarillo de Tormes and one of the many animals which have given its name to a civilization of the Meseta.

Opposite the Bull, Hannibal's Gate links the population with the struggles against Rome in the third century B. C., at a time when the Roman bridge was not yet a landmark on the road from Astorga to Mérida. Later, Moslems and Christians fought for the city until the eleventh century brought calm together with the person of Raimundo of Borgoña, son-in-law of Alfonso XI, who was to start its repopulation.

This is the period in which the Romanesque cathedral was started and all the churches that were built about this time in different parts of the town were of this style. The cathedral gave birth to an ecclesiastical school which, in its turn, was to culminate in 1218 in the formation of a University which throughout the ages has been renowned for the quality of both its professors and students.

The Renaissance was to mean cultural strength at the University, the new influence of art in architecture, religious ferment at the Council of Trent and in America, Portugal, Italy and Flanders in all of which illustrious men from Salamanca could be found.

The Baroque period brought some new ideas for the towers of the Clerecia and Cathedral and the arches of the Plaza, together with the decline of the University. The 19th century was a time of war and destruction; France, England and Spain were fighting in Ciudad Rodrigo, Los Arapiles and in Salamanca itself, where many parts of the city were razed by the cannons' bombardment.

To-day the University is flourishing once again; new sections have been inaugurated, new faculties and colleges opened, so that fresh intakes of students, who will fill the lecture rooms and those of the Pontifical University, can be accomodated.

Predominately a centre of agriculture and cattle-breeding, Salamanca has been slow to accept industry, perhaps because its lot has always been Armunian cereals and livestock to which can now be added the ever increasing number of tourists who come to visit the city.

Roman bridge over the Tormes.

THE GOLDEN STONE OF VILLAMAYOR

The character that historic cities acquire with time comes from that particular outline which makes them unmistakeable. Salamanca can see itself reflected in the river Tormes encircled by the Roman arches of the bridge, whilst beyond the Cross at Hannibal's Gate, the characteristic district of the tanneries, the two Cathedrals and the baroque bell-tower of the University complete those features that stand out against the blue sky.

But there is something different in the appearance of Salamanca that tells us that it is this city and no other that rises before us. It is the golden colour of the stone which is such a characteristic of the city's buildings.

Salamanca, the golden city, grew out of the mellow stone quarried at Villamayor, only four kilometres along the road to Ledesma. From these quarries came the stone which was used to give form to its dominating towers, its robust city-walls, the slender serrated edges of the Cathedral and the grotesques of the University. A visitor would be surprised to see the stone-mason hewing the stone with his axe or giving form to a moulding with his energetic rubbing of the mould on the damp stone. But the hammer and the chisel do not sing in the hands of one who is carving with them, and it is no secret why.

The stone of Villamayor, a silica-clay sandstone of very fine grain, is found on the edge of the Tormes or in very damp regions near to it. It retains the moisture of the quarry, which greatly facilitates the fine carving of the artists of Salamanca: when once it has dried out, it retracts and hardens. This is the secret of the "embroidery in stone" of San Esteban and of the facades of the Cathedral and University. This is the reason for which Salamanca is the plateresque city "par excellence".

With the passing of time, the pale colour of the hewn stone turns into a brilliant gold or golden red. But many suns must pass across these facades before the dusky and bloodlike reds acquire the patina which will gently ennoble the grotesques and coats of arms, the crests and pinnacles, the domes and towers of which, thanks to the generous quaries of Villamayor, there are many in Salamanca.

Detail of the University façade. ▶

ΟΙ ΒΑΣΙΛΕΙΣ ΤΗ ΕΓΚΥΚΛΟΠΑΙΔΕΙΑ· ΑΥΤΗ ΤΟΙΣ ΒΑΣΙΛΕΥΣΙ

FERDINAND   ELISABETH

Plateresque work on the Lower Schools.

Detail of the Cathedral. ▶

SANTA
BASILICA
CATEDRAL

THE MOST BEAUTIFUL SQUARE

Salamanca is the University and the Plaza Mayor. Even for those who find in the University the main focus of interest, the Plaza is also essential. As a place for a walk or a rendez-vous, it is indispensible. If, at the same time, it is artistic and uniform, you have something that is unique. It for this reason that it is the most beautiful square in Spain.

It came into being when the city required a conveniently sheltered place for a market. It was planned logically and tenaciously in a mildly but uniformly baroque style.

The City Council has kept the plans of Alberto Churriguera and the model for the Town Hall by Andrés García de Quiñcnes which provided for two domes, but in fact they were never built

In 172:) building started and it was to continue for twenty-five years. The east side was the first to take shape, and on this side stands out, above the Arch of the Bull (Arco del Toro), the so-called Royal Pavilion, from which kings watched exhibitions of horsemanship and bull-fighting. They continued with the south and west sides and the north was finally completed by the Town Hall. This is a baroque palace which runs the length of the square breaking its uniformity, but at the same time concentrating one's attention on that side cf the rectangle which is permanently in the sun. Besides those architects already mentioned, José de Lara, Nicolás Churriguera and Jerónimo García de Quiñones also played a part in the construction of the square.

Carvings on the spandrels of the arches along two sides of the square immortalize some of the great figures of Spanish history, whilst on the other two sides the coats of arms of the University, its Colleges, the Cathedral and the Nobility mark those ancient properties from the balconies of which pageants were watched, which to-day have been revived in the Festivales de España and which have for their beautiful setting and staging this illuminated square.

Being the pulse and life of the city, it receives everything of interest that comes to Salamanca. To this square come illustrious visitors, and from it depart official delegations and at its centre vibrates, throughout its ceremonies and pageants, the soul of the people of Salamanca.

In contrast to what has happened to many others, this square has remained lively and modern in spite of everything; it has always been preserved with love and attention, but it has never occurred to anyone to try and demote it to being merely a historic sight, always the prelude to worse things to come.

Now that you know something of the Plaza, you may enter Salamanca. The entrance-hall will help you to imagine the house.

◀ The Plaza Mayor of Salamanca.

Royal Pavilion of the Plaza Mayor.

4

VESTIGES OF ISLAM

In spite of being a considerable distance away from Andalucía and having been repopulated mainly by people from the North, many traces of the influence of Moorish art can still be found in Salamanca, an influence which must have been considerably greater in past times

The recent collapse, in 1963, of the Convent of Las Dueñas deprived us of two Moorish doors inlaid with tiles and Arabic stonework, the like of which do not exist in Sevilla or Granada according to Torres Balbás. A third door, which is not such a good example, remains intact near the entrance to the upper cloister and from this we are able to know something of what was the palace of the Contador Mayor of Castilla, Juan Sánchez, who brought some well-known craftsmen from Sevilla to carry out some modifications to his house before it was eventually given by his widow to the Dominican Mothers.

We find further examples of Moorish art on the ceiling of the great door of the University which faces the Cathedral and which used to be the site of the ancient chapel; the colourful ceiling is covered with intricate Arabic stonework and below it runs an ornamental frieze. The upper cloister also has a Moorish coffered ceiling, as does one of the old classrooms in the courtyard of the Escuelas Menores and the circular Romanesque church of San Marcos y Santa María de los Caballeros.

However, it is not common to find a Mozarabic frieze on a Christian tomb as can be seen on that of Chantre Aparicio in the wing of the transept of the Old Cathedral. It is also strange that the ancient chapter-house of the same cathedral, to-day the chapel of Talavera, should have a vault traced with parallel arches whose inspiration can undoubtedly be found in the art of the Moors.

It would also appear contradictory that what was the church of the Comendadoras of the Order of Santiago, today the parish church of Sancti Spíritus, should have a choir, now converted into the Chapel of Cristo de los Milagros, with coffered ceiling and side-walls of delicate Arabic tracery which is repeated on a small and rather unusual pulpit. Similar to this are the choirs of the Madres Isabeles and Ursulas and the organ in the Chapel of Amaya in the old Cathedral.

Beside the river, at the foot of the Roman bridge, a church dedicated to Santiago (St. James) was worked in brick in the Romanesque-Mudéjar style. Having been restored recently, it now possible to know what the builders were capable of doing in their efforts to try and copy the Romanesque techniques without the use of stone. It is the architectural proof that men from the South also took part in the repopulation of Salamanca.

◀ The *Ayuntamiento*, or town hall, on the north side of the Plaza Mayor.

Lace-like Moorish design in the University foyer.

Intricate ceiling of the Provincial Museum. ▶

Front of the Romanesque-*Mudéjar* Church of Santiago.

Clavero Tower. ▶

ART AT THE TIME OF THE REPOPULATION

The most ancient churches in the city belong to the Romanesque period. One must not forget that the repopulation af the city was carried out by Count Raimondo of Burgundy in the twelfth century, a time at which this style was widely prevalent. Although the passing of the centuries has deprived Salamanca of many of these primitive churches, there are still five which remain, without taking into account the Old Cathedral.

They are widely dispersed throughout the city as they were, in their day, the religious centres of the people who came to repopulate the city and these liked to live in groups according to their place of origin: there were peoples from the highlands and plains of Castilla, from Galicia and Portugal, Franks and Mozarabs and they all wanted to have their own place of worship.

Just off the Plaza Mayor and surrounded by other buildings is the Church of San Martín, which dates from 1103 and belonged to the people who had come from Toro. The north door is well preserved and the interior, which boasts three wide aisles, contains several pointed arches and some magnificent Gothic tombs.

San Marcos dates from 1178 and the exterior was originally of circular from. The interior consists of three aisles and three apses. The arches are pointed and it is topped by a baroque belfry.

The Church of Santo Tomás de Canterbury, which was put up by some English settlers soon after the canonization of Thomas Becket, dates from 1175; it has only a main nave and is at present being restored.

On the top of a hill, now in the heart of the city, the people of Toro built San Cristóbal in 1145. A part of the original vault, several capitals and the exterior of the apse are in good preservation, but the church is no longer used as a place of worship.

The Church of San Juan de Barbalos dates from prior to 1150. It can be found near to the Plaza de Santa Teresa and only possesses a single nave. It has recently been restored.

Lastly, near the river and facing Hannibal's Gate, is the Church of Santiago, built by the Mozarabs; this explains its architecture of brick in the Romanesque-Mudéjar style. Much of the original construction has been lost in its restoration.

It is noteworthy that in spite of the proliferation of the Romanesque, Salamanca lacks a cloister in this style. But there are very interesting remains in the Sacristy of the Fundación de la Virgen de la Vega, just beside the Tormes. There are several arches of great beauty and the capitals are most elegantly carved; these, like the rest, date from the twelfth century.

Romanesque-Moorish dome of the Talavera Chapel.

◀ Romanesque image of Our Lady of La Vega, patron saint of Salamanca.

Romanesque rotunda of San Marcos.

THE OLD CATHEDRAL

As if it wished to remain unnoticed, the Old Cathedral o Salamanca does not openly display the interesting features o its architectural style. The north side is completely hidden by the New Cathedral, and the original facade and tower were pulled down in 1679 on the orders of Bishop Seijas Losada who had them replaced in undistinguished Baroque by Setien Güemes

Seen from the Plaza of Juan XXIII, the dome of the transept, known as the Torre del Gallo (Tower of the Cock), stands out with its covering of scalelike stones similar to those of Périgueux, for its construction was begun by Bishop Jerónimo who came from that city. As it is masked by the new cloister it is necessary to pass along some typical sidestreets to reach the Patio Chico, a well-loved corner of Salamanca, from which it is possible to contemplate the elegantly traced Romanesque apses and the transept of the New Cathedral; from here also the Torre del Gallo can be seen to better advantage.

The architecture of the interior is the result of the transition that took place when the new techniques of the Gothic masters were replacing those of the Romanesque. The cruciform pillars and graceful capitals support a vault for which they were not designed. The problem of supporting the ribs of the vault has not been very successfully resolved, although more light was obtained by the use of high windows; but the original vault was lost and possibly also something of the elegance of the Torre del Gallo, but, in spite of everything, it still retains most of it.

Construction is generally considered to have been started by Bishop Jerónimo of Périgueux in 1140, that is soon after the repopulation of the town, but with the passing of time the plans were changed on many occasions and according to Dr. Camón up to six masters were put in charge of this work. In 1179 it was Pedro de la Obra, in 1182 Pedro Esteban was followed by Juan el Pedrero, in 1202 Pedro, in 1207 Sancho Pedro and in 1225 Juan Franco.

The original tombs at the foot the right aisle, the magnificent altar-piece by Nicolás Florentin who was also responsible for the Final Judgement painted on the vault, the dome of the transept and the paintings in the Chapel of San Martín greatly enrich the old See of Salamanca, as they are all exceptional if not unique.

Tower of El Gallo («The Rooster») on the Old Cathedral.

Apse of the Cathedral.

Interior of the Old Cathedral. ▶

Retable by Nicolás Florentino in the Old Cathedral.

Old Cathedral, interior of cupola.

Old Cathedral. Fresco in the apse showing the Last Judgment,
by Nicolás Florentino (Dello Delli).

Organ gallery in the Chapel of Los Anayas.

Detail of the tomb of *Doña* Elena in the Old Cathedral of Salamanca. ▶

Behind the transept door of the Old Cathedral we do not find the expected archway made up of matching columns because of modifications carried out in the 18th century which did away with the Romanesque cloister. When we go inside the Capilla de Talavera, a sarcophagus in the corner reminds us of an art that has disappeared.

This chapel was erected by Dr. Rodrigo Maldonado, a native of Talavera, who was an adviser to the Reyes Católicos (Ferdinand I and Isabella); he died in 1517. The chapel used to be the old chapter-house and dates from the 12th century. At its centre lies its founder, in front of an impressive reredos of the 16th century, on the right of which an inscription can be found alluding to a privilege which permits masses in the Mozarab rite to be celebrated at the altar. Perhaps this has some connection with the Moorish tracery that can be seen on the vault.

The spirit of the old University is revived when we contemplate the Chapel of Santa Barbara which dates from the year 1340. Here, with his back to the altar and his feet on those of Bishop Lucero —already much worn by the passing of students— an aspirant to a Doctorate passed a night of prayer and study awaiting the dawning of a day that would bring him before a tribunal that was to examine him in that very place. After the examination came triumph, a degree, congratulations and a visit to a bullfight. If he had failed, crestfallen and alone, he would have passed out of the door of the Carros (Carts) to face the possibility of a public mocking. Here, in this chapel, used to be the glories of Spanish culture, until the 19th century and its new methods reduced it to a museum and a memory.

Under the starred vaults of Santa Catalina, councils and assemblies gathered when Salamanca belonged to the arch-bishopric of Santiago. Here resounded the voices of the attorneys of Castilla and those of the defending counsel for the Knights Templar who were acquitted in this very chapel in the memorable Council of 1316.

Finally we come to the Chapel of Anaya, the mausoleum of the Anaya family, for which purpose it was erected in 1422 by Bishop Diego de Anaya, founder of the College of San Bartolomé; he lies in a fine tomb of alabaster under a beautiful vault in late Gothic style, surrounded by a railing which is the most impressive of its type. Here the Anaya family lie at rest in tombs built into the walls, whilst the spirit of the Council of Constanza seems to flow from the cardinal's hat and standard belonging to Anaya who announced to don Diego, before the Emperor Segismundo, that Castilla had recognized Martín V.

Santa Bárbara Chapel, where degree examinations were hold by the old
University. Old Cathedral.

Retable of Christ of the Battles, in the New Cathedral.

◀ Santa Catalina Chapel in the cloister of the Old Cathedral.

When Valencia was lost to the advancing Moorish troops, Jerónimo de Périgueux, Chaplain to the Cid, was installed as Bishop of Salamanca.

It is not generally known that in 1102 don Jerónimo took charge of the construction of the Old Cathedral. To him we also owe two most interesting documents which are now kept in the Diocesan Museum and which, without doubt, were brought to Salamanca during his tenure of office.

The first is a parchment in Visigothic characters, by which Rodrigo Díaz de Vivar made a donation in 1098 to the church of Valencia and its Bishop, Jerónimo. It closes with a confirmatory line in the hand-writing of the Cid which states "Ego Rudericus simul cum coniuge mea afirmo hoc quod superius scriptum est."

The other is also written in Visigothic characters and carries the date of 10th May 1101. We know from this document that doña Jimena, wife of the Cid, gave a tenth part of all she possessed to the church of Valencia, and she also ratified the previous donations of her husband. The confirmation, hand-written but now illegible, stated — "Ego eximina predicta qui hanc paginam fieri iussi manu mea confirmavi."

These important mementos of the Cid came to Salamanca with the beautiful Romanesque Christ, called "of the Cid" or "of the Battles", which is venerated in the central chapel of the presbytery of the new cathedral. This figure was the Christian symbol which showed the position of the Bishop, near to that of Díaz de Vivar (the Cid), in the battles, and probably comforted the Cid in his dying moments, as it is recorded that don Jerónimo was there to aid him at this time.

Below the altar of "Christ of the Battles" the remains of Bishop Jerónimo, so often mentioned in the Poem of the Cid, were laid to rest on his death in Salamanca on 30th June 1120.

Romanesque Christ of El Cid, also called «de las Batallas», «of the Battles».

THE UNIVERSITY TRADITION

More than seven hundred years existence is proof of a long University tradition which started when King Alfonso IX granted a founding charter to the Escuelas Salmantinas in 1218. Fernando III confirmed these privileges in 1243, as did also Alfonso IX in 1254, who, when doing so, already used the title of University; he also endowed it with professorships when Pope Alexander IV, comparing it to Oxford, Paris and Bologna, classified it as a centre of General Study.

These new privileges and grants take us up to the time of the Catholic Monarchs who were responsible for the starting of the new building, which is in the Patio de Escuelas, and has the most famous of all facades in the plateresque style; it is a real work of art in stone and the unique product of the quarries of Villamayor. It displays a combination of Italian and French themes and techniques, with heraldic, sculptural and bas-relief motifs, all worked with unequalled mastery and craftmanship.

A great increase in the number of students relegated this building to a more historic category, but it still contains the Grand Hall which is used for important academic ceremonies, the Chapel, with a reredos by Gavilán Tomé, in which the remains of Fray Luis de León are kept, the music room of the master Salinas, reception rooms and the old Theology School of Fray Luis which has been preserved in its original state. The famous staircase carved with Renaissance themes under a magnificent arched ceiling leads us to the old library behind whose Gothic doors are kept more than forty thousand volumes, five hundred ancient editions and three hundred manuscripts.

On the same floor, and facing it, is the modern library which contains over 165,000 volumes, and the Professors' Common Room which is decorated in the style of the 18th century.

The Rector's residence in the Patio de Escuelas now occupies the building that used to be the university hospital. The University Museum in the ancient Escuelas Menores contains canvases, carvings and panels under the ceiling of the old library, painted by Fernando Gallego. In other halls, the Historical Archives and those of the Municipality, together with the Archeological Museum, complete this original courtyard with its multistyled arches.

The old tradition of covering the walls of the ancient buildings with the names of graduates reddened with the blood of a bull mixed with olive oil has been resuscitated, and to-day the cloisters of the Faculties and the walls of the Colleges are painted in this way.

Façade of the University.

Dome of the University with its seal sculpted at the top.

Panegyric tablets in the University patio. ▶

Stairway in the University.

University classroom where Fray Luis de León taught. ▶

Old library
of the
University.

Front of the Arzobispo Fonseca *Colegio Mayor*.

THE OLD COLLEGES

The University has always been complemented by the Colleges and residences, in which the general education of the students was completed. Thery were not commonplace lodging-houses, but sumptuous edifices founded by important personages who entrusted them to well-known artists. Although there used to be many of them, only few have survived, and these are no longer used for the purpose for which they were founded.

The College of San Bartolomé or of Anaya was founded in 1401 and rebuilt in 1760 by Sagarvinaga and Hermosilla. To-day it is occupied by the Faculties of Letters and Science; in the residential part there is now a Teachers' Training College and the chapel is the parish church of San Sebastián.

The College of the Archbishop owes its existence to Alonso de Fonseca who founded it in 1519. Designed by Ibarra and realized by Covarrubias and others, it is one of the best examples of the plateresque style. It was used by Irish students during the 19th century and for that reason it is also called "Irlandeses". The courtyard is one of the best examples of the Spanish Renaissance and the original chapel has a reredos by Alonso Berruguete. The Aesidential part is by Churriguera and to-day houses the School of Medicine.

In the Paseo de Canalejas is the College of the Purísima Concepción, erected in 1603 by the Secretary of Paul III, Archbishop Solís y Quiñones, who was born in Salamanca. It is the work of Alberto Mora. The College of Carvajal, dating from 1662, can be found in the Plaza de Doyagüe.

The Inquisitor Valdés founded the College of San Pelayo in 1556. The only part that remains is the walls and these now enclose the University sports ground; the coat of arms of the founder can still be seen on the outside.

Calatrava dates from 1717 and is the work of Joaquín Churriguera: it is now the Diocesan Seminary. San Ambrosio, by Alberto Churriguera, was erected in 1720.

Within the orchard of San Esteban there are the remains of Santo Domingo, constructed by the Dukes of Béjar in 1533. It preceded the present Theological College of the Padres Predicadores de Salamanca.

The Royal College of the Holy Spirit, of the Society of Jesus, owes its existence to Margarita of Austria and her husband, King Philip III. Begun in 1617 by Gómez de Mora to accomodate 300 students, it is to-day part of the Pontifical University and comprises the buildings which surround the Church of the Clerecia.

In various parts of the city, the remains of other colleges can be found: for example Cañizares, San Ildefonso, Santa Catalina, Santa Maria de los Angeles, etc.

Gallery of the Arzobispo Fonseca *Colegio Mayor.* ▶

Front of the Espíritu Santo College, today Pontificial Ecclesiastical
University.

SHELLS AND FLEURS-DE-LIS

Among the many fine palaces of the city la Casa de las Conchas (the House of Shells) occupies a most important place, as much for the interesting period of its construction as for the originality and excellent taste of the unknown architect. Admiration for this delightful work of art has been unanimous at all times.

Deprived of its towers —it was once a stronghold— across the whole of its facade it is covered with numerous beautifully carved shells, the crest of the Pimentel Family, and the impressive coat of arms with its five fleurs-de-lis of the Maldonado family. Under the windows small figurines with laurels in their hands unite the shells and fleurs-de-lis in perpetual proclamation of the joining together of doña Juana Pimentel, daughter of the Condes de Benavente, and don Arias Maldonado, Comendador de Estriana and eldest son of Dr. Talavera Maldonado of the Royal Council of their Catholic Majesties, who prepared this house for her in about 1495. As time passed, the theme of the shells proved to be so attractive that it was repeated in 1701 by the then owner of the house, the Conde de las Amayuelas, when he enlarged the facade along the street called Rua.

Its iron grilles are considered to be the best of Spanish Gothic style. The windows at the corner of the building are embossed with iron family crests together with their motto and the Ave María, which is of the same period as the pomegranate of the royal coat of arms which dominates the facade.

The courtyard, one of the most elegant among the original series of Salmantine patios, is finished in open-worked and uninterrupted cresting of the fleurs-de-lis of Maldonado. Its varied coats of arms make up an authentic genealogy of the lineages joined together by marriage; including those of the exterior, they amount to 153 of Maldonado, Pimentel, Enríquez, Guzmán and Velasco. The unusual but characteristic reversed arches are repeated in the courtyard of the Escuelas Menores, in the higher cloister of the University and in the Palace of Fonseca, thus creating a style particular to Salamanca.

The harmonious uniformity, the intricate work surrounding the windows and the magnificent carving of the coats of arms, which on the main door proclaim the beginning of the plateresque style, ensure the superiority of this palace over that of Abarca. The House of Shells is considered the most beautiful civil construction undertaken by Spanish artists during the reing of Isabel la Católica.

Façade of the House of Shells.

Detail of the House of Shells. ▶

Patio of the House of Shells.

◀ Gothic grille of the House of Shells.

House of *Doña* María la Brava.

FACTIONS AND FEUDS

The Plaza de los Bandos, in the centre of the city, brings back to mind an era when the people of Salamanca were divided according to their dynastic preference and ancestry. The area now occupied by the central gardens was once the site of the Church of Santo Tomé in the shadow of which the Tomesine faction used to meet; whilst the Benitines used to gather on the boundaries of the parish of San Benito.

In a corner of the square, the house of María la Brava recalls a bloody feud between these two groups. Doña María, who came from the Enríquez de Sevilla family, had two sons who belonged to the Santo Tomé faction; they were murdered by the Manzanos, members of the group from San Benito, who immediately fled to Portugal. Doña Maria, being a widow, wished personally to avenge the death of her sons and pursued the murderers into Portugal, where she found them in Viseo. After cutting off their heads, she rode back to Salamanca and threw them on the tombs of ther two sons in the Church of Santo Tomé. From then on she has been known as "the Brave".

Later, in the reign of Carlos I, it was to be a representative of each of the two parishes who came to speak on behalf of the city before the central parliament of the Kingdom. And so Pedro Maldonado of San Benito and Antonio Fernández of Santo Tomé were received in audience by Mr. de Chievres, acting for the Emperor, and put forward the wishes of the people of Salamanca: among these figured the petition that the Emperor should not go to Germany to receive the Imperial Crown. The policies adopted by the Crown caused the uprising of the Communities or Municipalities amongst which could be found Zamora, Toledo, Segovia, Avila and Salamanca.

And so started the Movement of the Communities to which Salamanca contributed 200 pikemen and 600 footsoldiers. It continued until defeat came at Villalar, Francisco Maldonado and Pedro Maldonado Pimentel falling into royalist hands: they were executed together with Juan de Padilla from Toledo and Juan Bravo from Segovia. In the Chapel of Talavera in the Old Cathedral, which was founded by the grandfather of Francisco Maldonado, a purple standard with the armour of Maldonado Pimentel was kept and raised high, it is said, as a symbol to the followers of the Community of Salamanca.

Front of the Ursuline Church.

Exterior of the New Cathedral. ▶

If the Cathedral of León represents French Gothic at its purest in Spain, the New Cathedral of Salamanca demonstrates the characteristics of the end of this period when it had already started to decline. It was started in 1513, at a time when Bramante was already dead and León X was about to entrust the completion of the Vatican, in the new Renaissance style, to Michelangelo. The Chaper of Salamanca then commenced a Gothic cathedral that was to be, with that of Segovia and the unfinished one of Plasencia, the last to be built in Europe in this style.

Although it was realized that the old Romanesque Cathedral was very small, dark and low, no-one ever thought of pulling it down. A detailed plan for the new construction was necessary so that worship in the old should not be interrupted. Bishop Bobadilla, whose remains lie in the transept, was responsible for the new building.

Begun, strangely enough, at the foot, building gradually continued towards the transept and sanctuary, the original idea always being faithfully followed in spite of the succession of architects that followed Juan Gil de Hontañón. The plans were only changed by Rivero Rada, a pupil of Herrera, who adapted the polygonal sanctuary for the rectangular one it has to-day. Small details will tell us, however, how the construction advanced with time, for looking carefully one notices that the external cresting of the side-chapels and naves is in turn Gothic, Plateresque and finally Baroque.

Finally consecrated in 1733, the following masters were in charge of work in the 16th century —Juan Gil de Hontañón, Juan de Alava, Antón Egas, Rodrigo Gil de Hontañón and the above— mentioned Rivero Rada. The 17th century saw Juan Alvarez, Cristóbal de Honorato and Juan Setien in charge and then came the Baroque masters of the 18th, amongst whom figured the inevitable Churriguera who was responsible for the ancient dome which was changed for another in neo-classic style by Sagarvinaga. Devreton and García de Quiñones were responsible for the reinforcement of the original tower, the work of Pedro Rivero, which was badly damaged by the earthquake of 1755.

The few stained glass windows are by Nicolás de Holanda, Arce and Bro de Flandes. The magnificent facade with its bas-reliefs of the Birth and Adoration by Juan Rodríguez, who was also responsible for the Virgin and the Ramos facade, also contains work by Antonio de Malinas and Juan de Gante.

This is the artistic outline of a cathedral planned and built in the Gothic style, when the rest of Europe was firmly moving in the direction of the Baroque.

Front of the New Cathedral. ▶

Side of the New Cathedral.

Interior of the New Cathedral. ▶

Cupola of the New Cathedral.

Processional monstrance. ▶

MUSEUMS AND ARCHIVES

Salamanca, a city of monuments, lacks a first-class museum, as there is not one which possesses a completely representative collection. The whole city is a museum and it is, therefore, necessary to spend some time perusing a collection of works of art, the majority of which have remained in the setting for which they were originally created.

One could not imagine "la Inmaculada" by Ribera away from the reredos of the Augustinas, nor the reredos of Nicolás Florentín independent of the Old Cathedral; we could say the same of the Berruguete in the chapel of the Colegio de Irlandeses and of the Descent from the Cross by Juni in the cloister of the Cathedral.

However, for those works which for different reasons are not or cannot be in their original place, three small but select museums await the visitor.

In the cloister of the Old Cathedral, the Diocesan Museum contains panels and canvases of the 15th and 16th centuries besides Hispano-Arabic canvases and documents signed by the Cid.

In the courtyard of the Escuelas Menores, under the roof of the old university library painted by Gallego in 1494, the University has organized another collection of paintings on canvas and wood, also of the 15th and 16th centuries.

In the square of Fray Luis de León is situated the Palace of Abarca, a beautiful example of Gothic art at the time of Isabel la Católica and of the same style as the House of Shells, in which, on the ground floor, are kept stone figures, heraldic carvings and pieces of architectural interest taken from ancient buildings which have now either disappeared or been pulled down. On the first floor there are Flemish panels and paintings of different periods and schools, beside pieces of sculpture and ivory and examples of worked silver and gold.

Both the University and the Cathedral possess rich archives referring to their respective foundations in which can be found bulls, royal grants, warrants, etc., all of great interest.

Lastly, in the courtyard of the Escuelas Menores beside the University Museum, there are two archives; those of the Provincial History and Judicial Record and that of the Municipality of Salamanca, not forgetting those of the parishes and convents which, in some cases, are really notable.

Gothic palace of Abarca Maldonado. Today Provincial Museum.

The Planet Mercury, detail of the dome by Fernando Gallego, in the
University Museum.

Center
panel of
the San
Miguel
retable, by
Juan de
Flandes,
in the
Diocesan
Museum.

Everything in Salamanca is carvings and sculpture: the whole city is the product of hammer and chisel whether it be in its facades or interiors. After stading astonished before the facade of San Esteban wondering, before such creative ability, what can await us within, we enter and are met by the authentic "cascada" of carved wood of the main reredos and those of the side chapels. The same thing occurs in the University, the New Cathedral, Sancti Spíritus, las Dueñas, Corpus Christi, Clerecía and San Martín.

The inexhaustable variety of crests would make a decorated album of beauty and art. Outstanding are those of the Palace of Fonseca, the courtyard of the Irlandeses, the Casino, San Boal and the Plaza.

The heraldic carvings are unique, as can be seen in the Palace of Monterrey, Garci Grande, Abarca Maldonado, Solis and in the Houses of las Muertes, María la Brava, las Conchas, on the facade of Corpus Christi and those in baroque style on the sides of the Plaza Mayor.

The plateresque facades, looked at with binoculars, offer a spectacle of limitless variation, above all those of the University, San Esteban, the New Cathedral and Sancti Spíritus. They are so changed when looked at in this way that they appear completely different places.

Sculpture in wood, although not so fine or abundant, does not, however, lag so far behind. In the "golden chapel" of the New Cathedral alone there are more than a hundred pieces. In other chapels works by Gregorio Fernández, Mitatta, Salvador Carmona, Benlliure, Velasco de Sande, Juan de Juni, Carnicero and Churriguera can be seen, not forgetting the Romanesque Christ in the Chapel of the Battles. The Old Cathedral, besides the fine capitals of the nave and the tombs in the transept, also possesses the Romanesque Virgen de la Vega and some Limoges metal plaques that are almost the only ones in Spain: ther are also the carved tombs of the cloister and chapels.

The choir-stalls in the Cathedral are the work of Lara Churriguera and Alejandro Carnicero, and those of San Esteban were carved by Araújo and Balbás. Salamanca also possesses images (holy figures) by Felipe del Corral and Carnicero in la Vera Cruz, by Felipe de Borgoña in the University Museum, by Carmona and Pitti in la Clerecía, by Chapuz, Finelli and Algardi in la Purísima, by Mena in San Julián, by Andrés Paz in Sancti Spíritus, another by Carnicero in San Benito, by Giralde de Bruselas in the Chapel of Talavera and by Ceroni and Sardiña in San Esteban, which also contains the most beautiful Inmaculada by Gregorio Fernández.

Romanesque figure of Christ in the Sancti Spiritus Church.

Pietà by Salvador Carmona, in the New Cathedral.

Relief of the descent by Juan de Juni in the cloister of the Old ▶
Cathedral.

FRESCOS, PANELS AND CANVASES

In the Chapel of San Martín, in the Old Cathedral, there are some murals signed by Antón Sánchez of Segovia dating from the 13th century (1262) which are considered the best by a known artist of their style and period —a good beginning to an account of pictorial works which will include frescos, panels and canvases.

In the same chapel there are other murals of 1300 and 1340. On the tombs in the transept of this cathedral there are interesting compositions of the Epiphany and the Coronation of the Virgin which will be of interest to anyone studying the painting of León and Castilla. We continue with the panels and frescos of the reredos and vault of the main chapel by Nicolás Florentino, and then to the cloister in which can be found panels of the 15th and 16th centuries by Gallego, Pedro Bello, Juan of Flanders and the Master of Terradillos.

In the New Cathedral there are canvases and panels by Navarrete (known as the "Dumb"), Morales, Francisco Camilo, Espinosa and others attributed to Becerra, Sacchi, Titian and the Flemish School.

There are works by Cacianiga, Ferro, García and Vicente González in the University Chapel. The Church of la Purísima can be considered a pictorial museum for the works of the great Ribera, Guido Reni, Baglioni, Lanfranco and Bassano, whilst San Esteban is the same for Claudio Coello, Carmen de Abajo, Villamor, Palomino, Pitti, Pelegrín Tibaldi and Rubens, if the small painting of the Virgin in the choir has been rightly attributed; the copper plates in the sacristy could possibly oe by the same hand.

Conca and Orrente have left canvases in San Sebastián, Nicolás Florentino in las Isabeles, Martín Cervera in San Julián and the University Library, together with all those already mentioned in connection with the museums.

◀ Sculpture in the Church of Santa María de los Caballeros.

Painting by Antón Sánchez in the San Martín Chapel of the Old
Cathedral.

Painting of the Visitation by Nicolás Florentino, in the retable of the ▶
Old Cathedral.

Anyone who looks at the fine Plateresque facades of the University, San Esteban or Sancti Spiritus will understand that it is not a pure architectural style, but a form of decoration derived from the addition of Italianate motif to Gothic structure — this is the essence of the Plateresque style.

There is no relation between the facade and the interior of Sancti Spiritus; the nave is Gothic, as it also is in San Esteban: the same is true of the University with its arched interior. But whether it is a style or not, it is certain that, with the fair stone of Villamayor, a pleasing result has been achieved. Nor is it less certain that without the artists Salamanca gave birth to, the result would have been equally different.

There is nothing like the "embroidered" marvel of San Esteban and the University. In the first the majesty of its grand proportions is contrasted against a delicacy of detail, whilst in the second all is detailed work and precision, so much so that the observer does not notice the lack of windows.

However this style is not only for great buildings: it is also suitable for a nobleman's house, such as that of Diego Maldonado by the Church of San Benito, or the modest Convent of Corpus Christi.

A list of all the examples of Salamantine Plateresque would prove irritating; however, besides those already mentioned, one cannot omit las Dueñas, the door of the Escuelas Menores, the Palace of Solis, the Houses of Ibarra (las Muertes) and Garci Grande, the Palaces of Monterrey and Fonseca (now the County Council) and Rodriguez Figueroa (now the Casino). On another scale are the College of the Archbishop, also known as Irlandeses, which used to de the church of the Bernardas, and the facade of San Martin in la Quintana.

Nearly all Salamanca is plateresque in style, as if the colour and properties of the stone were made to receive the creative imprint of the artist.

In 1524 Juan de Alava began the Church of San Esteban of the Dominican Order. Planned in Gothic style, its facade is a triumphal arch covered with crests, sculptures and coats of arms. The central group and the carving of San Esteban were carried out by Ceroni in 1610. After the death af Alava, Rivero Rada continued the work: the happily resolved dome is repeated in the Chapel of the Irlandeses.

The loggia leading to the Convent, with its arches and crests, seems to have been brought there from some Italian Renaissance city: but, for being none the less of Salmantine style, it is not out of tune with the excessive decoration of the grand facade.

Front of the Sancti Spiritus Church. ▶

Pilaster and bas-reliefs on the façade of the Church of San Esteban.
Plateresque details of San Esteban.

◀ Façade of the Church of San Esteban.

Capital in the cloister of the Convent of Las Dueñas.

◀ Details of the Church of San Esteban.

Monterrey
Palace.

THE PATIOS OF SALAMANCA

It is a pleasure to devote an after-noon to exploring the patios of Salamanca. However, a day would not be sufficient to get to know those which in Salamanca are considered important or famous. The small ones, hidden away and silvent, are legion.

That of the House of Shells (las Conchas) could be a good way to start off seeing how the Moorish influence in its low arches contends with the Italianate capitals of the upper gallery, whilst the Gothic parapet blends in with the Renaissance laurel surrounds of the coats of arms. The whole is, without doubt, Spanish in style, notwithtanding the openworked fleurs-de-lis which might suggest something of French origin to those who had forgotten that it was the Maldonado crest.

In the patio of the Escuelas Menores a repetition of the arches will be found, but the technique is better. The finish of the balustrade and torchbearers is more modest but less intimate: it is not in vain that it was built to hear the bustle of students.

In the upper cloister of the University the same style of arches is repeated, and by now it has been perfected. The atmosphere is severer and more propitious to higher studies.

Complete equilibrium has been attained in the Patio de Irlandeses or College of the Archbishop, in which harmony and proportion seem to have joined hand in hand. In this the sun also plays its part, as its arches are made more golden by it in this than in any other of the city's courtyards with the exception of the Plaza Mayor, which is rather like a patio common to all the inhabitants of Salamanca.

In the patios of San Boal and Arias Corvelle the line is classical and they are famous for their crests and carved stairway.

The patios of the Dominican convents are also worth a visit. That of San Esteban is a complete museum of sculpture and a new conception in cloisters, in tone with the facade. The coat of arms of the Bishop of Toledo, in appearance rather like a chess-board, is repeated on the walls, on the doorways into the garden and below the intricately arched ceiling. At the other side of the small bridge is the Patio de las Dueñas which is, without doubt, the best and the most surprising of Salamanca's patios, and which in itself would make a visit to the city worthwhile. The high gallery, with its capitals and lintels marvellously carved in a variety of themes of constant originality, is quite unique.

The Palace of Anaya is also suprising for the architraves of its gallery in which a grey-coloured stone is contrasted with the more pleasing golden sandstone. The stairway is like that of a great palace.

Lastly, the baroque patio of the Clerecia, with its gigantic columns, is a splendid example of the art of the Counter-Reformation.

◀ Upper cloister of the Dominican Convent of Las Dueñas.

Patio of the old Lower Schools of the University.

Neoclassical patio of the old San Bartolomé or Anaya College.

Patio of the Clerecía, today Pontifical University. ▶

Nearly the whole of Salamanca consists of small streets. The many fine buildings that it possesses hinder urban development which always comes to a stop before some facade tower or building of particular interest.

The lay-out of the streets appears therefore rather old, for there are many corners and quiet little places such as the Patio Chico, the Park of San Francisco, the Patio de Escuelas, the Plaza (Square) de los Sexmeros and of Santa Teresa, each one of which has its own special atmosphere. The square of Santa Teresa, with the stone column at its centre, recalls the many communities founded by the restless Saint. The shady little corner of the Ursulas seems to contemplate the figure of the Patriarch Fonseca whose tomb is in the convent founded by him, and that of Unamuno whose house, in the Palace of the Regidor Ovalle, is beside that of the Muertes.

If from here we continue towards the south we will pass in front of the ancient Church of Santa Maria de los Caballeros, the Tower and Palace of Monterrey and the Convent of the Augustinas, until we arrive at the Convent of the Mother of God (Madre de Dios). Here we find the "corner" of San Benito, surrounding the church of the same name which was restored by Fonseca. Opposite the apse is the plateresque house of Diego Maldonado, the church's faithful servant. Beside it is the Palace of Solis, a lineage so widely spread throughout Salamanca that it is rare not to find coats of arms which do not contain its sun. When we come out again into the street of la Compañia, an edifice similar in style to that of the Escorial tells us that we are in front of the College of the Holy Spirit, the site of the Pontifical University, to which the baroque Church of la Clerecia gives an unmistakable outline.

Opposite the dome of la Clerecia, the street called Libreros takes us past the University, the Patio de Escuelas and the Corral de Guevara, before coming to the College which was called Santa Maria de los Angeles, and Hannibal's Gate in the district of the Tanneries where the old houses are adorned with lintels which proclaim the names of their owners. Opposite we find the Bull and the Roman bridge, and not far away the Romanesque Mudéjar church of Santiago.

The little streets round the Cathedral lead to the Patio Chico. In the centre of the city the Square of San Boal guards the legend of the Marquise who came back to life. The calle del Prior (Prior Street) starts in Monterrey and ends in the Plaza Mayor. Near is the Corrillo de la hierba with its dramatic memories. Tentenecio is another typical corner of the old Salamanca, which so faithfully guards the character of its houses, the tranquility of its patios, and the surprises of its most characteristic little "corners".

◀ Patio of the House of the Doctors.

Calle de Libreros.

Torre del Aire («Tower of Air»). ▶

PALACES AND COATS OF ARMS

The list of palaces emblazoned with their coat of arms is a long one. It is difficult to put them into groups as each one has its own characteristics.

Monterrey justifies its position at the head of the list as it is the most prodigal in blazonry which can be seen on its towers, windows and chimneys: the coats of arms include those of Acevedo, Fonseca, Zúñiga, Biedma, Ulloa, Maldonado, Sotomayor and Castro, all united in what is to-day the ducal House of Alba.

More urban in character is the Palace of Garcigrande in the Plaza de los Bandos which has a plateresque facade carrying the arms of Spinosa, Girón, Guzmán and Maldonado, all of which have been joined together in the Viscountcy of Garcigrande. Fonseca is the name of the facade of what is now the County Council; the chields in the patio which date from the recent restoration face the tormented figures which, supporting the upper gallery, give the patio, open under great arches supported by brackets, its particular character. The palace of Solís, extremely simple in style, is on the corner of San Benito: under its own shield there are two more with the families Zúñiga, Maldonado, Rodriguez, Anaya, Monroy Abarca and Díaz de Ledesma represented. Beside it the House of Diego Maldonado, servant of the Patriarch Fonseca, unites the five stars of the prelate with the Maldonado, Medrano and Morille lineages.

The small square of San Boal is decorated with the shields of two palaces and a church. When rain wets the stone it is still possible to see the faint coats of arms of what was the palace of Rodriguez de Ledesma y Figueroa, but now serves as the Casino.

Only the shields remain of the palace in which Felipe II married María of Portugal, which used to be beside the present Telephone Exchange; this has a window which displays the shields of Rodriguez, Solís, Monroy and Rodríguez de las Barrillas.

The shield on the house of Unamuno is that of the Governor Ovalle. The Palace of Orellana in the street of San Paulo has coats of arms of the Anaya Family, whilst those on the Palace of Abarca, in the square of Fray Luis, are of the Abarca and Alcázar families.

Some of the family names of Salamanca do not lack royal ancestry. Enriquez de Sevilla, together with Monroy and Maldonado, are on the house of María la Brava as her husband was a descendent of the Infante Henry, son of Fernando III. The Portuguese Quinas appear on the church of Sancti Spiritus and the arms of England quartered with those of Toledo can be seen on one of the properties belonging to the Alba estate on the old road to Villamayor.

Fonseca or Salina Palace (Provincial Government). ▶

Patio of Fonseca Palace, today seat of the provincial government.

Maldonado coat of arms, House of Shells.

NOBLE TOMBS

Many fine artists, most of them unknown, have enriched the art of the city by their contribution to its mausoleums and tombs, etc. A most interesting series starts with the tombs at the foot of the Old Cathedral; one can then proceed to the extraordinary Gothic ones of the transept before reaching the main chapel. In the chapels of the cloister there are tombs of all types, culminating in those of the Anayas.

In the New Cathedral the tomb of Bishop Bobadilla, its founder, stands out: it can be found in the transept.

The Church of the Isabeles is the pantheon of the Solís family, whilst San Martín possesses, amongst several, the most beautiful Gothic tomb, that of a knight named Ruperto Santiesteban who lies under an engrailed arch on a tumulus with angels supporting his family crest: Profesor Camón relates his position to that of the Doncel de Sigüenza. The Maldonados, under their fleurs-de-lis, are laid to rest in San Benito, whilst in Sancti Spiritus, unnoticed, lies the Infante Martín Alonso, son of Alfonso IX and his wife María Meléndez.

The Counts of Monterrey are buried in the chapel of the Augustinas, being the founders of the convent and church.

But there are four tombs in Salamanca which are fragments of Spanish history. One, in the chapel of Anaya in the Old Cathedral, carved in alabaster in Italian-Burgundian style, is the burial place of Archbishop Anaya, founder of the College of San Bartolomé, who took part in the Council of Constanza: he died in 1437.

Another in the Ursulas, magnificently carved in marble seemingly bq Diego de Siloé, is of Alonso de Fonseca, patron of Renaissance art, friend and protector of Erasmus, Archbishop of Santiago and of Toledo, who, being Primate of Spain, baptised Felipe II: he died in 1512.

The third is of the Grand Duke of Alba, Fernando of Toledo. He lies in the Sanctuary of San Esteban; although the tomb has little artistic merit, being neo-Gothic of the 19th century, it reminds us that Fernando was beside the Emperor Charles in Tunis and that he accompanied him throughout Europe. He was best man at the marriage of Felipe II in Salamanca, and his adviser in Englad: as Commander of the Royal Troops, he fought in Hungary, La Goleta, Rosellón, Mühlberg, Milán, Brussels, Harlem and Lisbon. He died in 1582.

Finally in San Julián, the tomb of Dr. Ramos del Manzano tells us that he was an adviser to the Holy Office of the Inquisition, President of the Royal Council of the Indies and Italy, also of Castilla, a representative of Felipe IV at the Treaty of the Pyrenees, acting a professor of the University of Salamanca: he died in 1671.

Gothic-Arab tomb of the precentor Aparicio in the Old Cathedral. ▶

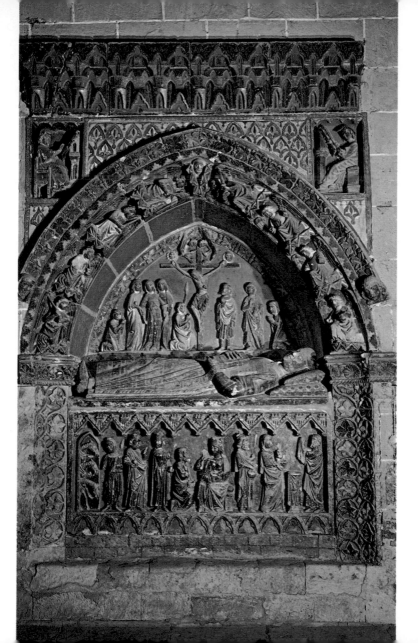

Tomb in Anaya Chapel in the Old Cathedral.

◀ Tomb of *don* Alonso de Fonseca, Patriarch of Alexandria, in the
Ursulina Church.

Tomb of Dr. Ramos Manzano, in the Church of San Julián.

A VICEROY'S FOUNDATION

The Viceroy of Naples, Manuel de Fonseca y Zúñiga 6th Count of Monterrey, founded the convent of the Augustinian Mothers. He was a noteworthy person both on account of the way he discharged his duties in Italy and because he was married to Leonor de Guzman, sister of the Duke of Olivares.

During his period of office in Naples he became a friend of the great painter José Ribera who, in 1635, had already painted for him la Purisima: he decided to donate it to Salamanca and as a suitable setting he built the Church of the Augustinas, although its foundation can also be attributed to a desire that one of his daughters should enter the convent.

The construction was begun by Bassano in 1636, the Spaniards Hoya, Gómez de Mora and Desculte also taking part. Bassano's inspiration gave to Salamanca the only Spanish-Italian church in the style of Vignola. Its wide nave culminates in the great dome of the transept, definitively the work of Setien Güemes.

Looking down from a reredos worked in fine marble is the great canvas painted by Ribera "The Immaculate Conception", surrounded by works by Lanfranco, Guido Reni and Baglioni. Along the walls of the main chapel we find the praying statues of the Counts, the work of Algardi and Finelli. The facade with its Italian style marbles displays a baroque coat of arms of similar design to that situated under the pulpit of the church, also of marble. Other reredoses in the church are decorated with canvases such as the San Jenaro by Ribera, the Crucifixión by Basano and the Annunciation by Lanfranco.

Opposite the church, the palace constructed in 1539 by the third Count of Monterrey, Alonso de Acevedo, explains the construction of the church on ground which belonged to the palace. This seigniorial mansion occupies only one side of the great square that had been planned. Its towers are the most beautiful example of their style in Spanish Renaissance architecture and are the work of Gil de Hontañón, Brother Martin of Santiago and the Aguirres.

Although the cresting, chimneys and pillars are exceptional, they are nothing compared with the shields and their supports which proclaim the eight lineages which, in the 16th century, were joined together in the earldom — Acevedo, Fonseca, Ulloa, Maldonado, Biedma, Zúñiga, Sotomayor and Castro.

Church of the Augustinian Order.

THE DAWN OF BAROQUE

Salamanca, to a greater extent than most cities, had felt much in harmony with the Plateresque style and for this reason it is so characteristic of its art. However, when the time came, it knew how to identify itself with those new styles which to-day attract the attention of lovers of art.

It started with the Glerecía, begun by Gómez de Mora, with the easily recognisable Herrera lines of its interior and lateral facade. However, as soon as Father Matos was put in charge of the construction in 1655, the new Baroque style made its appearance, and this was reaffirmed even more strongly by the new architect, Peña de Toro. But it was to be when the latter went to Santiago in 1652, when the new style of the Clerecía was included in the plans for the belltower of the Obradoiro in that town, that the most important step forward was achieved. And when another Jesuit, Father Bautista, was searching for inspiration for the new Jesuit church in Madrid, it will be clear to many that in the building of San Isidro we have another variant of the great work in Salamanca.

With this formula decided upon, it was to be the general pattern for Jesuit churches, although not all of them attained such a complete identification with the baroque style as the towers of Salamanca, which came from an unfulfilled plan by García de Quiñones for the Town Hall which dominantes the Plaza Mayor. Its appearance from the street of Palominos could not be bettered, even by a great square.

The reredoses, together with the inter-play of light and shade obtained from the windows and great lantern contrasting with the obscurity of the side-chapels, combine to give the baroque characteristics to an ambitious undertaking which occupies an area of more than three thousand square metres. Such a vast project would never have been possible without the initiative and continuous support of Margaret of Austria, wife of Philip III, who in 1617 took a special interest in its completion.

But our idea of the Clerecía would be incomplete without knowings something of its great courtyard, considered by Schubert to be one of the most perfect Baroque creations to be found in any country. Profesor Camón believes it to be the work of García de Quiñones and has no doubt in classifying the whole as architecturally the most spirited, the most grandiose and the most abundant in baroque feeling of all Spanish works of art.

◀ The Immaculate Conception in the principal retable of the Augustinian convent church, today the Purísima parish church, one of José de Ribera's finest works (1635).

A FAMILY OF ARTISTS

As a result of characteristic Spanish individualism, the culminating moment of Baroque art was baptised "Churrigueresque". For this reason Churrigueresque and Baroque are synonymous, although in the world of art the reality is probably somewhat different.

Of Catalan origin, but for some time resident in Madrid, the Churriguera family moved to Salamanca at the beginning of the 18th century, where they were to leave many works which would link their name with the town. It is rare to find a building without a reredos, a facade, some modifications or at least documentation telling of something done by them. Also things have been attributed to them that they did not do and in some cases the coincidence of name and a lack of proof has meant that works by one or other Churriguera have been confused.

José Benito Churriguera was the creator of the great reredos of San Esteban in 1693. The grandeur of his style is in keeping with the cathedral-like proportions of the temple. The hostel of the College of Anaya, to-day a Teachers'Training College, with its patio that is a baroque versión of the plateresque of the Irlandeses, is the work of his brother Joaquin, as are also the College of Calatrava and the dome of the New Cathedral which had to be demolished as a result of the earthquake of 1755. Also attributed to him are the interior of la Vera Cruz and the presbytery and reredos of Christ of the Battles in the New Cathedral.

His brother Albert left his imprint on the choir of the New Cathedral, on the College of San Ambrosio, on the Church of San Sebastián with its beautiful doorway in the square of Anaya, on the reredos of San Martín and on the present-day Faculty of Medicine. The house of the Rector of the University is also attributed to him, but there are those who believe it is the work of Manuel Lara Churriguera. Because of his differences with the architect Ribera over the construction of the tower of the Cathedral, he was forced to leave Salamanca in 1738.

We close the family cycle with the above-mentioned Manuel Lara Churriguera, a sculptor and nephew of Joaquin. He was responsible for the bookcases of the old library of the University, the ante-chamber to the Sacristy of the New Cathedral and the plans for the Sacristy which were later put into effect by Sagarvinaga. In cooperation with Alejandro Carnicero he also contributed to its carved choir-stalls.

These are the achievements of a family who were not natives of Salamanca, but who, as a result of the quality and continuity of their work throughout, a century, left an indelible mark on it.

◀ Main façade of the Clerecía.

Side door of the Church of San Sebastián.

◀ Principal retable in the Church of San Esteban, a work by José de Churriguera.

Details of carving in choir, done by Lara Churriguera and Alejandro Carnicero.

◀ Front of San Sebastián.

The boroque interior of Vera Cruz.

PLAZA DE ANAYA

Beside the Cathedral there is a quiet little corner of the city which is almost the private courtyard of the University, as around it there are three of its four Faculties: one could say that it almost exists for the happy bustle of students. On arrival, one is impressed by the golden mass which is the Cathedral.

A modest garden containing a statue to Bishop Cámara forms the centre-piece of the square which is the least homogeneous of the city, although it does not lack a certain charm. As you look round the square you will see the great Cathedral contrasting with simple dwellings, whilst between the two is the palatial-looking College of Anaya.

From the Ramos door of the New Cathedral, the simple facade that the University presents on this side seems to evoke the protection bestowed on it by kings and popes: the blazons of León and Castilla and of Pope Luna can be seen carved above the door, whilst the two smaller ones of Tostado seem to symbolize the intelligence of those who were its professors. And as if this facade were really a symbol, two inscriptions on it summarize the two most characteristic facets of the city —Culture, in the motto "OMNIUM SCIENTIARUM PRINCEPS SALMANTICA DOCET" under the University seal, and Tourism, foretold by Cervantes when he put into the mouth of one his characters that "SALAMANCA ENHECHIZA LA VOLUNTAD DE VOLVER A ELLA A TODOS LOS QUE DE LA APACIBILIDAD DE SU VIVIENDA HAN GUSTADO" (Salamanca attracts in a way that makes all those who have enjoyed its pleasant atmosphere wish to return).

The narrow street named after the lawyer Vitoria passes in front of the Law Faculty and comes out opposite the dome and towers of the Clerecia, whilst the street called Rúa, much frequented by students, connects the Plaza de Anaya with the Plaza Mayor, masking one side of the baroque church of San Sebastián which was once the chapel of the College of San Bartolomé, also known as Anaya. In the latter are now the Faculties of Letters and Science, whilst on the right-hand side of its neo-classic facade its old hostel has been turned into a school for teachers.

A good symbol of what were the past glories of the University Colleges, this building provides a better close to the Plaza: facing the Cathedral, it contrasts with the side below the gardens where the characteristic houses of the streets of El Silencio and El Tostado make it difficult to see the plateresque marvel of San Esteban.

Old Anaya College, today Faculty of Letters.

Plaza de Anaya.

...que al ponerse
tras las encinas que el celaje esmaltan
dora a los rayos de su lumbre el padre
Sol de Castilla:
bosque de piedras que arrancó la historia
a las entrañas de la tierra madre,
remanso de quietud, yo te bendigo,
!mi Salamanca!"

This is the way in which Unamuno saw the poetic outline of Salamanca from the Park of San Francisco: for from there he saw a sea of domes and twin towers on which the sun of centuries has left its mark. Before him seemed to rise up those of La Clerecía, the Cathedral, Las Agustinas and the three of Monterrey together with the distant El Aire and the bold cupola of the Ursulas.

These lofty towers formed, as it were, a drop-curtain in the life of Unamuno who came to identify himself fully with University and local life, just as if he had been born beside the Tormes.

His name remains united to that of Salamanca, where his memory is kept alive in the Rector's House, now converted into a museum and place of work. There, beside the historic University, the baroque facade of the street of Libreros is the faithful custodian of his memory.

And not far away, in the Plaza de Anaya, the Faculty of Philosophy and Letters proudly displays a magnificent bust by Victorio Macho: it has been placed at the top of the great staircase out of perpetual respect for a man who was one of its most illustrious professors. Anyone who wanders admiringly through the streets of this art-filled city will come to the ancient palace of the Regidor Ovalle, opposite the convent of the Ursulas. It was the last residence of don Miguel and in it, shortly before his death, he wrote a last poem that was almost a presentiment:

"Morir soñando, si; mas si se sueña
morir, la muerte es sueño; una ventana
hacia el vacio; no soñar; nirvana;
del tiempo al fin la eternidad se adueña."

Sculpture of Unamuno by Pablo Serrano. ▶

Old Rector's Home, today Unamuno Museum.

THEY PASSED THIS WAY

Every house and street of Salamanca suggest the presence of great figures from history, from art and from science.

After the Cathedral had been founded, the University became the focal point of the city. The great figures who would, as time passed, be drawn towards it by reason of its wide renown make up an unending list: only those of most distinction would fill many pages, the more so if we take into consideration those who were not notable here, but were to be so after finishing their studies in the old Colleges and lecture-rooms of the University of Salamanca. Marineo, Sículo, Anglería, el Tostado, Nebrija, Arias Montano, el Brocense, Fray Luis de León, Melchor Cano, Vitoria, Zacut, Juan del Encina, Saavedra Fajardo, Tirso de Molina, Cervantes, Lope de Vega, Góngora, Garcilaso, Torres Villarroel and Unamuno are sufficient for a start.

The struggles of the Reconquest brought Alfonso I, Alfonso II and Ramiro III to either occupy or defend the city. Here Alfonso XI was born, Prince Juan died, Felipe II married, Fernando the Catholic lived and Carlos I, Felipe III and Felipe V came. Here also Hernán Cortés studied and Christopher Columbus discussed.

San Juan of Sahagún, San Vicente Ferrer, San Ignacio de Loyola and Santa Teresa de Jesús passed through Salamanca. The first brought peace to the afore-mentioned disputing factions and left us his patronage and ashes. The voice of the second was heard in fervent prayer, whilst convents witnessed the passing of the other two.

Alba de Tormes and El Huerto de la Flecha have many memories of Spanish theatre, literature and poetry. Salamanca was the scene of, or served as an inspiration for, several literary compositions: the Roman bridge in "Lazarillo de Tormes", "La Celestina" a picaresque character of Salamanca, "Las Batuecas" a comedy by Lope de Vega, and "La Cueva de Salamanca" a work by Cervantes.

A city of art "par excellence", Salamanca was moulded by those geniuses who have carved out its features from the time of the Roman bridg up to the present day: amongst these figure Covarrubias, Bigarny, Alava, los Egas, Ibarra, the Hortañons, Orozco, Rasines, the Churrigueras, Quiñones, Siloé, Mora and many others who have constructed towers, carved facades, cloisters and palaces in a city which contains one of Spain's most interesting collections of buildings and monuments.

Monument to Fray Luis de León, by Nicasio Sevilla.

Cloister of San Esteban.

THE LEGEND OF THE HOUSE OF THE DEAD

When people pass in front of the pleasant-looking Casa de las Muertes (House of the Dead), they often ask the reason for its name. A vague and evasive answer is always given, as very little is known about it. It is possible that its origin comes, not from the house itself, but from the street in which it is, as there is documentary proof that in 1753 it was called the "street of the dead".

One explanation was published in 1898 by the scholar Bolanegra according to which a love affair between two members of the Monroy and Manzano families, great rivals in the Salamanca of the 15th century, led to the death of two people. When, many years later, this house was being built, the bodies were found between the stones of some foundations together with another two without heads which were said to be those of the Manzano brothers, decapitated by María la Brava. This is a neat story which links the tragedy of the "factions" with that of the "dead".

Another versión states that a priest's family was murdered in this house. Others say that the name is derived from the skulls which have been carved between the windows by way of decoration, a motif much used in the plateresque style; they had been converted into balls, but in 1964 the original motif was reintroduced.

The facade is a splendid example of the Salmantine plateresque style: its decorative panels and crests reveal a great artist. The coats of arms, the compasses over the door, and the polite deference of the two people who are showing a shield to Archbishop Fonseca lead us to believe that it could have been the house of the architect Ibarra, who was responsible for most of the constructions put up in Salamanca by Fonseca, Patriarch of Alexandria. The five stars of Fonseca do not, however, appear: this refutes the idea that it could have belonged to him, as is commonly claimed.

After having had a link with the Ibarra family up to 1805, the house was then sold by public auction as a result of the Royal Decree of the 19th September 1798 which ordered the disposal of Church possessions; this it had become by way of a donation.

House of Death.

As it has remained tied to its traditional preferences for the University, agriculture and livestock, Salamanca has not experienced that unrestrained drive towards modernisation which has been distinctive of the industrial nuclei. For this reason it has kept its own way of life which continues in characteristic streets full of history, of which the Plaza Mayor is a good example.

But this does not mean to say that Salamanca has not felt the wind of change of modern times: opinions expressed by people who have been away from the city for some time testify to the radical changes that have taken place during their absence. However, Salamanca, faithful to the works of art it possesses, does not break up its own features, but as someone enthusiastically said, it has been reborn within itself. In the middle of the 20th century one can therfore see the plateresque style again being used for buildings in the Calle del Concejo and for a bank in the Calle de Zamora which copies the nearby Palace of Rodríguez Figueroa, whilst in the Plaza de los Bandos the Palace of Garci Grande was used as a model for the Telephone Exchange and the Social Security Centre; the same thing occurred in the case of Glorieta Barracks and the Palace of Monterrey. Shortly afterwards the Gran Vía was opened in order to allow traffic to flow more freely from north to south of the city, and for the central part a mixture of mild baroque and neo-Isabelian was used, perhaps due to the influence of the Torre del Aire which is close-by.

The central part of the city, bounded by the Paseos Canalejas, San Vicente, Carmelitas and Avenida de Mirat, keeps its golden colour as all buildings are still constructed with special stone. When once the line of the ancient wall had been broken, the expansion that followed was responsible for the creation of a new city on the northern side, possibly attracted by the railway station as well as the desire to get away from the river which then was not regulated, as to-day, by a flow of water from the reservoir of Santa Teresa de Villagonzalo.

The straight avenues of Federico Anaya, Torres Villarroel and Portugal form the axes of the new residential city; the flat western part is traversed by the Avenida Brunete, and the lively Avenida de Italia also belongs to this district. High modern blocks of flats with a new architectural line contrast with the neighbouring ancient part, where the two Cathedrals and the Plaza Mayor remain typical of a city that has not renounced its inheritance from a glorious past.

We therefore have two cities which make up the modern Salamanca: one is full of art and history, whilst the other organizes industrial estates and, slowly but surely, brings new ideas to a people who know how to respect the old.

Avenida de Portugal. ▶

Fresco of the Church of El Arrabal, by Genaro de No.

◀ Church of Our Lady de Fátima.

The Square of Santa Teresa, dominated by a stone column indicating the ancient jurisdiction of the Herrera Anayas, founders of the now non-existent Convent of the Bernardas, was once a tranquil place; this peace has now been threatened by an increase in traffic and the announcement of its pending modification.

In this square is the house which used to belong to the Ovalles, relatives of Santa Teresa. She stayed there when she came to Salamanca in 1570 with Sister María del Sacramento to found communities such as that of the Carmelite nuns on the road to Villamayor. In this house, in 1571, she experienced one of her ecstasies; it is therefore almost certain that some of her inspired works were also written there. The room that used to be hers is now the chapel of the Servers of Saint Joseph, who look after the house.

Alba de Tormes was also favoured by the foundation of a convent in 1571, and on the road from Salamanca a fountain commemorates her having passed along that road on her way to the ducal estate: there, at the petition of her relatives, the Ovalles Ahumada, and supported by the Dukes of Alba, she founded anther convent. Many years later, in 1582, Santa Teresa returned to her convent at Alba de Tormes and died there on October 4th.

Her remains are kept behind a fine silver grille in the main reredos of the church, in a chest donated by Isabel Clara Eugenia, daughter of Felipe II. Her heart and an arm are also exposed there for the veneration of the faithful. One can also see the room in which she died and the place where her body lay before being taken to its final resting place.

Alba de Tormes, besides the notable connections it has with Santa Teresa, also possesses interesting Romanesque-Mudéjar churches such as San Juan and Santiago, in which can be found impressive reredoses and tombs. There is also a tower of the ancient palace of the Dukes which contains recently restored pictures. In the days when messengers from the Imperial Court used to arrive at the castle and new works by Lope de Vega were performed for the first time inside its walls, this was the political and cultural centre of Spain.

Other convents in the town, and that of San Jerónimo nearby, continually recall the name of Alvarez de Toledo: the remains of the Grand Duke used to be kept in the latter until they were moved to San Esteban in Salamanca.

Our Lady of Sorrows, by Pedro de Mena, in the Discalced Carmelite Convent in Alba de Tormes.

◀ Alba de Tormes. Carmelite Church.

THE PROVINCE OF SALAMANCA

A large extension of fields and ilex woods, the principal product of which is bulls bred for the bull-ring, covers the south and west of the province, to which the N-620 road to Portugal provides an axis. Here, in an extensive area of grazing pastures, it is not difficult to see young bulls being tested for their courage in the ring.

But not all the province is the same : to the north and east of the capital is La Armuña, a hard dry land where cereals are grown. La Sierra follows the northerly peaks of the Central Range which here is made up of the Béjar and Gata Sierras and the great peak of Peña de Francia on the top of which, at 1724 metres, is the Dominican Sanctuary bearing the same name. Los Arribes is an impressive rocky land through which flows the Duero on the border with Portugal ; in its protected valley grow agaves and prickly pears, almonds and olives, oranges and lemons because at the foot of the Saucelle dam the altitude is only 112 metres compared with an average for the province of 700 metres. Further up the river there is a fall of water which is the highest in Western Europe, that of Aldeadávila which is of 140 metres.

When looking at a map of the province the town of Béjar, a textile centre, stands out, whereas Ciudad Rodrigo, a walled seigniorial town, together with La Alberca and San Felices de los Gallegos, has been declared a centre of history and art. Ledesma, Alba, Monleón, Tamames, Miranda del Castañar, El Tejado Sobradillo, Puente del Congosto and Montemayor still have their ancient walls or castles, but none of them are as welcoming as those of Ciudad Rodrigo and Villanueva de Cañedo which have been converted into modern hotels.

In the folds of the hills up in the Sierra there are villages full of tradition and character, such as Candelario and La Alberca, Villarino and Miranda, Monleón, Robleda and Sequeros and in some of them it is not unusual to see the older members of the village going about their daily tasks in the traditional costumes of the region.

A province of contrasts, Salamanca is suitable for fishing or shooting, art or history, folklore or industry ; it possesses also a cultural focus in its capital and a religious focus at Alba de Tormes, seat of Spain's most famous duchy.

Rural scene in the province of Salamanca. ▶

Market day in the Plaza de Peñaranda in Bracamonte.

A street in La Alberca. ▶

Traditional dress of La Alberca.

◀ Panoramic view of Béjar.

Aerial view of Ciudad Rodrigo.

Detail of the upper part of the southern wall of the Cathedral of Ciudad Rodrigo.

◀ The three columns that symbolize the city.

View of the aisle of the Cathedral. Ciudad Rodrigo.

Castle of Enrique II, today a *parador* for tourists. Ciudad Rodrigo.

The *Ayuntamiento*. Ciudad Rodrigo.

Apse of the Church of San Pedro. Ciudad Rodrigo.

Cattle fair. Ciudad Rodrigo.

The running of the bulls. Ciudad Rodrigo.

INFORMACION PRACTICA SALAMANCA
INFORMATION PRATIQUE SALAMANQUE
PRACTICAL INFORMATION SALAMANCA
PRAKTISCHE HINWELSE SALAMANCA

Para cualquier otra información puede Vd. dirigirse a la Oficina de Turismo de esta localidad, sita en: Gran Vía, 11.

Pour toute information, vous pouvez vous adresser au Bureau du Tourisme de cette ville, situé: Gran Vía, 11.

For further information, visit the Tourist Office in this town, located at: Gran Vía, 11.

Zur Erhaltung irgendeiner anderen Auskunft können Sie sich an das Turismusbüro dieser Ortschaft in der Gran Vía, 11.

1. ARTE Y CULTURA
ART ET CULTURE
ART AND CULTURE
KUNST UND KULTUR

1.1. CONJUNTO MONUMENTAL Y MUSEOS
ENSEMBLE MONUMENTAL ET MUSEES
MONUMENTS AND MUSEUMS
SEHENSWURDIGKEITEN UND MUSEUM

SANCTI SPIRITUS. *SANCTI SPIRITUS.*
SANCTI SPIRITUS. *SANCTI SPIRITUS.*

Iglesia siglo XVI, interior gótico, exterior rena-
contiota italianizante. Interesantes tumbas y
retablos. Capilla del Cristo de los Milagros,
con artesonado morisco (siglo XVI).

*Eglise du XVIe siècle; intérieur gothique, exté-
rieur renaissance italienne. Tombeaux et re-
tables intéressants. Chapelle du Christ des
Miracles, plafonds mauresques lambrissés
(XVIe siècle).*

XVIth century church; gothic interior, italianized Renaissance exterior. Interesting tombs
and altarpieces. Chapel to «Cristo de los Milagros» (Christ of the Miracles) with Moorish
caissoned cieling.

*Kirche XVI. Jahrhundert; Innenraum gotisch,
Aussenseite italianisierter. Renaissance-Stil.
Interessante Grabmäier und Altaraufsätze.
Capilla del Cristo de los Milagros mit moris-
kem Täfelwerk (XVI. Jahrhundert).*

TORRE DEL AIRE
TOUR DE L'AIR
TORRE DEL AIRE.
LUFTTURM

Antiguo palacio de los Fermoselle, de airosa
silueta italianizante, con bellos ajimeces y to-
zas góticas del siglo XV.

*Ancien Palais des Fermoselle à l'élégante sil-
houette de style italien; belles fenêtres citrées
et sculptures gothiques en bois du XVe siècle.*

Former palace of the Fermoselle family, with a
graceful Italianized outline, beautiful mullion-
ed windows and farters of the XVth century.

*Alter Palast der Familie Fermoselle, anmutige
italianisierte Silhouette mit schönen geteilten
Bogenfenstern aus dem XV. Jahrhundert.*

PLAZA MAYOR.
GRAND' PLACE.
PLAZA MAYOR. *PLAZA MAYOR.*

La más bella de las plazas porticadas españo-
las; barroco (siglo XVIII). Destacan el lado
Norte (el Ayuntamiento), y el Este (el llamado
Pabellón Real).

*La plus belle des places à portiques espagno-
les; baroque du XVIIIe siècle. Le côté nord
(Mairie) et l'est (appelé Pavillon Royal) sont
remarquables.*

The most beautiful of all Spanish portico squa-
res; baroque (XVIIIth century). The North side
(the City Hall) and the East Side (The so
called Royal Pavilion) are noteworthy.

*Der schönste der spanischen Plätze mit Säu-
lengang; barock (XVIII. Jahrhundert). Die
Nord- (Rathaus) und Ostseite (der soge-
nannte Königliche Pavillon) stechen hervor.*

SAN MARTIN. *SAINT MARTIN.*
SAN MARTIN. *SAN MARTIN.*

Iglesia románica (siglo XII). Portada románica
al Norte y plateresca al Sur. Ventana barroca
del siglo XVIII.

*Eglise romane (XIIe siècle). Portail roman au
nord et plateresque au sud. Vitrail baroque
du XVIIIe siècle.*

Romanesque Church (XIIth century). Romanesque façade on the North side and plateresque in the South. XVIIIth century baroque
window.

*Romanische Kirche (XII. Jahrhundert). Nord-
portal romanisch, Südportal plateresk. Ba-
rockes Fenser aus dem XVIII. Jahrhundert.*

PALACIO DE LA SALINA O DE FONSECA.
PALAIS DE LA SALINA OU DE FONSECA.
PALACIO DE LA SALINA OR DE FONSECA.
PALACIO DE LA SALINA ODER DE FONSECA.

Edificado en 1538. Airosa fachada; patio con
arcos, capiteles y ménsulas de gran interés.
Hoy es Diputación Provincial.

*Construit en 1538. Façade élégante; cour à
arcs, chapiteaux et encorbellements intéressants. Héberge aujourd'hui la Députation
Provinciale.*

Bult in 1538. Graceful façade; courtyard with
arches, capitals and corbels of great interest.
It is now the Provincial Deputation.

*Erbaut 1538. Anmutige Fassade; Innenhof mit
sehr interessanten Bögen. Kapitellen und
Kragsteinen. Heute Sitz des Provinziallandt-
tags..*

PALACIO DE ORELLANA.
PALAIS DE ORELLANA.
ORELLANA PALACE.
PALACIO DE ORELLANA.

Señorial mansión representativa del estilo intermedio entre final del renacimiento y co-
mienzos del barroco (siglo XVII).

Hôtel seigneurial représentatif du style intermédiaire entre la fin de la Renaissance et le début du Baroque (XVII).

Lordly mansion, an example of the intermediate style between the end of the Renaissance and the beginning of the Baroque (XVIIth century).

Herrschaftlicher Wohnsitz kennzeichnend für den Übergangsbaustil zwischen Ausgang der Renaissance und Anfang des Barocks. (XVII. Jahrhundert).

TORRE DEL CLAVERO.
GARDIENS DES CLÉS.
KEEPER OF THE KEYS TOWER.
TURM DEL CLAVERO.

Perteneció al Clavero de la Orden de Alcántara, don Francisco de Sotomayor. Resto de su casa señorial. Reúne el interés de la fortaleza militar y la belleza constructiva del siglo XV. Visita: exterior solamente.

Appartenait au Gardien des Clés de l'Ordre d'Alcántara, Francisco de Sotomayor. Vestige de sa demeure seigneuriale. Unit l'intérêt de la forteresse militaire à la beauté architectonique du XVe siècle.

Owned by the Keeper of the Keys of the Order of Alcántara, Francisco de Sotomayor. The remains of his lordly mansion. It unites the interest of the military fortress and the constructive beauty of the XVth century.

Gehörte dem Clavero des Ordens von Alcántara, Don Francisco de Sotomayor. Uberrest eines herrschaftlichen Hauses. Interressant als Kriegsfestung sowie bauliche Schonheit des XV. Jahrhunderts.

SANTO TOMAS DE CANTERBURY.
SAINT THOMAS DE CANTERBURY.
ST. THOMAS OF CANTERBURY.
SANTO TOMAS DE CANTERBURY.

Iglesia románica erigida en 1175 por dos maestros ingleses; es la primera del mundo dedicada al Santo de su nombre, Tomás Becket. Contiene interesantes sepulcros.

Eglise romane construite en 1175 par deux maîtres d'oeuvre anglais: c'est la première au monde dédiée au Saint dont elle porte le nom Thomas Becket. Contient d'intéressants sépulcres.

Romanesque church built in 1175 by two English architects; it was the first in the world to be dedicated to the Saint, Sir Thomas Becket. It contains interesting sepulchres.

Romanische Kirche, die im Jahre 1175 von zwei englischen Baumeistern errichtet wurde; die erste der Welt, die diesem Heiligen Thomas Becket, gewidmet wurde. Enthält interessante Grabmaler.

ANTIGUA IGLESIA DE LAS BERNARDAS.
ANCIENNE EGLISE DES BERNARDINES.
FORMER CHURCH OF THE BERNARDINES.
ALTE KIRCHE DER BERNARDAS.

Hoy se halla en el interior del nuevo convento de los Padres Escolapios. Comenzada en 1552 por Gil de Hontañón, puede considerarse como prototipo de los templos salmantinos del siglo XVI.

Se trouve aujourd'hui à l'intérieur du nouveau couvent des PP. Escolapiens. Comencée en 1552 par Gil de Hontañón, elle peut être consideree comme le prototype des sanctuaires de Salamanque du XVIe siècle.

It is to be found today inside the new convent of the Escolapian Fathers. Begun in 1552 by Gil de Hontañón, it can be considered a prototype of the XVIth century churches in Salamanca.

Heute befindet sie sich im Innenraum des neuen Klosters der los Padres Escolapios. Gil de Hontañón begann im Jahre 1552 mit den Bauarbeiten. Die Kirche kann als Prototyp der salmantinischen Kirchen des XVI. Jahrhunderts betrachtet werden.

CALATRAVA. *CALATRAVA.*
CALATRAVA. *CALATRAVA.*

Edificado en 1717 por Joaquín Churriguera, modificada por Jovellanos en 1790. Perteneció a las Ordenes Militares. En la actualidad es sede del Seminario Diocesano.

Construit en 1717 par Joaquin Churriguera, modifié par Jovellanos en 1790. Appartenait à l'Ordre Militaire de ce nom. C'est actuellement le siège du Séminaire Diocésain.

Built in 1717 by Joaquín Churriguera, modified by Jovellanos in 1790. It belonged to the Military Orders. At present it is the seat of the Diocesan Seminary.

Im Jahre 1717 von Joaquín Churriguera erbaut; im Jahre 1790 von Jovellanos baulich verändert. Gehörte den Militärs-Orden. Heute bildet sie den Sitz des Diözesan-Seminars.

SAN ESTEBAN. *SAINT ETIENNE.*
SAN ESTEBAN. *SAN ESTEBAN.*

Monumental portada plateresca. Interior de finales del gótico. Frescos de Palomino y Villamor. Gran retablo de Churriguera, con pintura de Claudio Coello. Interesante claustro.

Portail plateresque monumental. Intérieur de la dernière époque gothique. Fresques de Pa-

lomino et Villamor. Grand rétable de Churriguera, peint par Claudio Coello. Cloître intéressant.

Monumental plateresque façade. Interior end of gothic period. Palomino and Villamor frescos. Great Churriguera altarpiece, with Claudio Coello painting. Interesting cloister.

Monumentales platereskes Portal. Innenraum stammt aus dem Ende der Gotik. Freskomalereien von Palomino und Villamor. Grosser Altaraufsatz von Churriguera mit Malerei von Claudio Coello. Interessanter Kreuzgang.

DOMINICAS.
COUVENTS DES DOMINICAINES.
DOMINICAS, DOMINICAS.

Edificio de 1533, con portada plateresca. Interior de finales del gótico. Claustro renacentista de gran interés. Abierta al público, de marzo a octubre.

Bâtiment datant de 1533, portail plateresque. Intérieur dernière époque gothique. Cloître renaissance de grand intérêt.

Built in 1533, with façade. Interior end of gothic period. Renaissance cloister of great interest.

Erbaut im Jahre 1533, mit platereskem Portal. Innenraum Ende der Gotik. Hochinteressanter Kreuzgang im Renaissance-Stil.

PALACIO DE ANAYA. *PALAIS D'ANAYA.*
ANAYA PALACE.
PALACIO DE ANAYA.

Antiguo Colegio de San Bartolomé, hoy Facultad de Filosofía y Letras. Estilo neoclásico, comenzado en 1760. Interesante patio y escalera con busto de Unamuno, por Victorio Macho, en el rellano.

Ancien collège de Saint Barthélemy; abrite aujourd'hui les Facultés des Sciences et Philosophie et Lettres. Style néoclassique; commencé en 1760. Buste de Miguel de Unamuno par Victorio Macho.

Former college of St. Bartholomew, today Science and Philosophy and Letters Faculties. Neoclassical style, begun in 1760. Bust of Miguel Unamuno by Victorio Macho.

Altes Colegio von San Bartolomé, heute Naturwissenschaftliche und Philosophische Fakultäten. Neoklassischer Stil; Baubeginn 1760. Büste von Don Miguel de Unamuno von Victorio Macho.

CATEDRAL NUEVA. *NOUVELLE CATHEDRALE.*
NEW CATHEDRAL. *NEUE KATHEDRALE.*

Iniciada en 1513 por Gil de Hontañón, trabajaron J. Alava, R. Gil, Ibarra, Rivero Rada, los Churriguera y Sagarvinaga, y se terminó en 1733. Portada principal, alarde de ornamentación y composición.

Commencée en 1513 par Gil de Hontañón; J. Alava, R. Gil, Ibarra, Rivero Rada, les Churriguera et Sagarvinaga y travaillèrent aussi, et elle fut achevée en 1733. Le portail principal est un chef-d'oeuvre d'ornementation et de composition.

Begun in 1513 by Gil de Hontañón and worked on by J. Alava, R. Gil, Ibarra, Rivero Rada, the Churrigueras and Sagarvinaga and it was finished in 1733. Main façade a display of ornamentation and composition.

Baubeginn 1513 unter Gil de Hontañón; ferner arbeiteten J. Alava, R. Gil, Ibarra, Rivero Rada, die Churrigueras und Sagarvinaga; Baubendigung 1733. Hauptportal ein Renommierstück an Ornamentik und Komposition.

CATEDRAL VIEJA Y PATIO CHICO.
LA VIEILLE CATHEDRALE ET LE PETIT CLOITRE.
OLD CATHEDRAL and SMALL COURTYARD.
ALTE KATHEDRALE UND PATIO CHICO.

Románica, iniciada en el siglo XII. Retablo mayor de Nicolás Florentino (siglo XV). Famosa Torre del Gallo. Museo Diocesano. Desde el Sur se contempla el llamado «Patio Chico».

Romane; commencée au XII° siècle. Rétable principal de Nicolás Florentino (XV). Fameuse Tour du Coq. Musée Diocésain. Du sud, on contemple le «Petit Cloître».

Romanesque, begun in the XIIth century. High altarpiece by Nicolás Florentino (XVth century). Famous Torre del Gallo (Cock's Tower). Diocesan Museum. From the south side one can look at the so called «Patio Chico».

Romanisch, Baubeginn XII. Jahrhundert. Hauptaltaraufsatz von Nicolás Florentino (XV. Jahrh.) Berühmter Torre del Gallo (Hahnenturm). Diözesan-Museum. Von der Südseite betrachtet man den sogenannten Patio Chico.

IGLESIA DE SANTIAGO.
EGLISE DE SAINT JACQUES.
CHURCH OF JAMES
KIRCHE VON SANTIAGO.

Siglo XII. En ladrillo estilo románico-mudéjar.

XII° siècle. En briques, style roman-mudéjar.

XIIth century. In brick, Mudéjar-Romanesque style.

XII. Jahrhundert. Backsteinbau im romanischen Mudéjar-Stil.

VERRACO Y PUENTE ROMANO.
PONT ROMAIN.
ROMAN BRIDGE. *RÖMISCHE BRÜCKE.*

El toro o verraco ibérico es aludido en «El Lazarillo de Tormes» y hoy forma parte del escudo de la ciudad. El puente se halla en la
vía romana de Mérida a Astorga («Calzada de
la Plata»). Son de factura romana los quince
arcos del lado de la ciudad, habiendo sido
restaurados los restantes. Se desconoce la
fecha exacta de su construcción.

*Probablement construit par Trajan. Desservait
la chaussée romaine d'Astorga à Mérida
(chaussée d'Argent). Taureau ibere à l'entrée
nord, mentionné dans le «Lazarillo de Tormes».*

Probably built by Trajan. Used as Roman High
way from Astorga to Mérida (Silver Highway).
Iberian Bull at north entrance mentioned in
the novel «Lazarillo de Tormes».

*Walhrscheinlich Trajano zu verdanken. Diente
de römischen Heerstrasse von Astorga nach
Mérida (Calzada de la Plata). Am Nordein-
gang iberischer Stier, der auf den Lazarillo
de Tormes (Blindenführer vom Tormes) an-
spielt.*

UNIVERSIDAD. *UNIVERSITE.*
UNIVERSITY. *UNIVERSITÄT.*

Fundada por Alfonso IX de León, en 1218. Es la
más antigua de España. Su fachada pasa por
ser la más bella del plateresco. Busto de los
Reyes Católicos y escudo de Carlos V. En su
interior, «Aula de Fray Luis de León», Capilla
e interesantísima Biblioteca. Escalera con re-
lieves en antepechos. Claustro superior con
riquísimo artesonado.

*Fondée par Alphonse IX de León en 1218. La
plus ancienne de l'Espagne. Sa façade est
considérée comme la plus belle du plateresque. Buste des Rois Catholiques, armoiries
de Charles V. A l'intérieur, «Salle de Fray
Luis de León». Chapelle et Bibliothèque ex-
trêmement intéressantes, escalier avec ba-
lustrades à reliefs. Le Cloître supérieur est
magnifiquement lambrissé.*

Founded by Alfonso IX of León in 1218. It is the
oldest in Spain. Its façade is considered the
most beatiful example of plateresque; Bust of
the Catholic Kings and shield of Charles V.
Inside «Fray Luis de Leon's» classroom.
Chapel and very interesting library and stairs
with breastwork reliefs. Uppercloister with
rich porticoes.

*Im Jahre 1218 von Alfons IX, von León gegrün-
det. Es ist die älteste Universität Spaniens.
Ihre Fassade gilt als die schönste im plateresken Stil: Büste der Katholischen Könige
und Wappen Karls V. Innerhalb des Gebäu-*

*des Aula de Fray Luis de León. Kapelle und
hochinteressante Bibliothek sowie Treppe
mit Reliefs in der Brüstung. Hochkreuzgang
mit reichem Täfelwerk.*

ESCUELAS MENORES. *PETITES ECOLES.*
LOWER SCHOLS. *ESCUELAS MENORES.*

Portada plateresca. Bellísimo patio, de arcos
mixtilíneos, típicamente salmantinos. Museo
(Pintura, «Cielo de Salamanca», Arqueología).
Archivo Municipal e Histórico Provincial.

*Portail plateresque. Très belle cour avec arcs
mixtilignes typiques de Salamanque. Musée
(Peinture, «Ciel de Salamanque», Archéologie). Archives Historiques Municipales et
Provinciales.*

Plateresque façade. Very beautiful courtyard,
with mixtilineal arches, typical of Salamanca.
Museum (Painting «Sky of Salamanca», Archeology). Municipal and Historical Provincial Archives.

*Platereskes Portal. Sehr schöner Innenhof mit
originellen Rundbögen, typisch salmanti-
nisch. Museum (Gemälde, Himmel von Salamanca, Archäologie). Stadt- und historisches
Landesarchiv.*

MUSEO PROVINCIAL. *MUSEE PROVINCIAL.*
PROVINCIAL MUSEUM. *LANDESMUSEUM.*

Antigua casa del doctor Alvarez Abarca, mé-
dico de Isabel la Católica. Edificio típicamente isabelino (siglo XV).

*Ancienne demeure du Docteur Alvarez Abarca,
médecin d'Isabelle la Catholique. Bâtiment ty-
piquement de l'époque (XV⁰ siècle).*

Former house of the Dr. Alvarez Abarca. (Isabel
la Catolica's doctor). Typical Isabeline style
brilding (XVth century).

*Altes Haus des Doktors Alvarez Abarca, Arzt
Isabellas von Kastilien. Gebäude im typischen isabellinischen Stil (XV. Jahrh.).*

CASA DE LAS CONCHAS.
MAISON DES COQUILLES.
HOUSE OF SHELLS.
CASA DE LAS CONCHAS.

Fines del siglo XV. Considerada como el monumento más representativo del arte civil de
los Reyes Católicos. Interesantísimas rejas,
consideradas como las mejores del gótico
español. Bellísimo patio.

*Fin du XV⁰ siècle. Considérée comme le mo-
nument le plus représentatif du génie civil
des Rois Catholiques. Intéressantes grilles
considérées comme les plus belles du gothique espagnol. Très belle cour.*

End of XVth century. Considered the most representative monument of civil art of the Catholic Kings. Very interesting grilles, considered the best examples of Spanish gothic. Very beautiful courtyard.

Aus dem Ende des XV. Jahrhunderts. Wird für das kennzeichnendste Monument der zivilen Baukunst der Katholischen Könige gehalten. Hochinteressante Fenstergitter, die als die besten der spanischen Gotik bezeichnet werden. Sehr schöner Innenhof.

CLERECIA.
EGLISES AUX CLERCS
CLERECIA. *CLERECIA.*

Comenzada en 1617 por iniciativa de Felipe III y su esposa. La iglesia es de estilo intermedio entre el herreriano y el barroco. Junto a la iglesia, espléndido patio barroco de la Universidad Pontificia.

Commencée en 1617 à l'initiative de Philippe III et de sa femme. L'Eglise est d'un style intermédiaire entre le style d'Herrera et le baroque. A côté de l'église, la splendide cour baroque de l'Université Pontificale.

Begun in 1617 on the initiative of Philip III and his wife. The church is in an intermediate style between Herrerian and Baroque. Close to the church, splendid baroque courtyard the Pontifical University.

Baubeginn 1617 auf Initiative Philipps III, und seiner Gemahlin. Übergangsepoche zwischen Herrera-Stil und Barock. Naben der Kirche barocker Innenhof der Päpstlichen Universität.

SAN BENITO. *SAINT BENOIT.*
SAN BENITO. *SAN BENITO.*

Iglesia del siglo XV. Portada gótico-isabelina. Alrededor de este templo se hallan las casas de Solís y Maldonado de Morille; son ejemplos de casas platerescas de la primera mitad del siglo XVI.

Eglise du XVᵉ siècle. Portail gothique-isabellein. Autour de l'église, les demeures de Solis et de Maldonado de Morille son des exemples de bâtiments plateresques de la première moitié du XVIᵉ siècle.

XVth century church. Gothic Isabelline façade. Around this church, the houses of Solis and Maldonado de Morille are examples of plateresque houeses of the first half of the XVIth century.

Kirche aus XV. Jahrhundert. Gotisch-isabellinisches Portal. Umgeben von den Häusern von Solis und Maldonado de Morille, die Beispiele der plateresken Häuser der ersten Hälfte des XVI. Jahrhunderts darstellen.

PALACIO DE MONTERREY.
PALAIS DE MONTERREY.
MONTERREY PALACE.
PALACIO DE MONTERREY.

Construido en 1539, es el más característico de los palacios renacentistas españoles.

Construit en 1539, c'est le plus caractéristique des palais espagnols de la Renaissance.

Constructed in 1539, it is the most characteristic of Spanish Renaissance palaces.

Erbaut im Jahre 1539. Der bezeichnendste spanische Palast der Renaissance.

IGLESIA DE LA PURISIMA.
EGLISE DE LA VIERGE TRES PURE.
CHURCH OF THE VIRGIN MARY.
KIRCHE DE LA PURISIMA.

Comenzada en 1636, es la iglesia española de su siglo que más se ajusta a las normas artísticas italianas. En el Altar Mayor el bellísimo cuadro de la Asunción, de José Ribera.

Commencée en 1636, c'est l'église espagnole de cette époque qui s'approche le plus des normes artistiques italiennes. Au maître autel, magnifique tableau de l'Ascensión par José Ribera.

Begun in 1636, it is the church of its century which is the most adjusted to the Italian artistic standars. At the high altar the very beautiful painting of the Assumption, by José Ribera.

Baubeginn 1636. Es ist die spanische Kirche dieses Jahrhunderts, die sich am meisten den Normen der italienischen Kunst anpasst. Hauptaltar mit dem sehr schönem Gemälde «Mariä Himmelfahrt» von José Ribera.

COLEGIO DEL ARZOBISPO FONSECA O DE LOS IRLANDESES.
COLLEGE DE L'ARCHEVEQUE OU DES IRLANDAIS.
THE ARCHBISHOP'S OR THE IRISH COLLEGE.
COLEGIO DEL ARZOBISPO ODER DES LOS IRLANDESES.

Siglo XVI. Interesante fachada; iglesia con buen retablo de Alonso Berruguete. Uno de los patios más bellos del renacimiento español.

XVIᵉ siècle. Façade intéressante; église avec beau rétable d'Alonso Berruguete. Une des plus belles cours de la Renaissance espagnole.

XVIth century. Interesting façade; church with a good altar piece by Alonso Berruguete. One of the most beautiful Spanish Renaissance court yards.

XVI. Jahrhundert. Interessante Fassade. Kirche mit Altaraufsatz von Alonso Berruguete. Einer der schönsten Innenhöfe der spanischen Renaissance.

CASA DE LAS MUERTES.
MAISON DES MORTS.
HOUSE OF DEATHS.
CASA DE LAS MUERTES.

Ornamentación plateresca, que se supone debida a los artífices de la fachada de la Universidad. Medallón y efigie de don Alonso de Fonseca, patriarca de Alejandría.

Ornements plateresques atribuées aux auteurs de la façade de l'Université. Médaillon et effigie d'Alonso de Fonseca, patriarche d'Alexandrie.

Plateresque ornamentation, wich is assumed due to the artists of the University façade. Medalion and effigy of Alonso de Fonseca, patriarch of Alexander.

Plachereske Ornamentik, von der man annimmt, dass sie aus der Hand der Urheber der Universitätsfassade stammt. Medaillon und Bildnis von Don Alonso de Fonseca, Patriarch von Alexandrien.

CONVENTO Y MUSEO DE LAS URSULAS.
COUVENT DES URSULINES.
CONVENT OF THE URSULAS.
KLOSTER DE LAS URSULAS.

Primera mitad del siglo XVI. Iglesia con interesante torreón. Enclavado en un bellísimo rincón donde se encuentra también la Iglesia de la Vera-Cruz. Pequeño, pero interesantísimo Museo.

Première moitié du XVIᵉ siècle. L'église a un donjon intéressant. Située dans un très beau site, où se trouve aussi l'église de la Vera-Cruz.

First half of XVIth century. Church with interesting turret. Situated in a beautiful corner, together with the Vera-Cruz Church.

Aus der ersten Hälfte des XVI. Jahrhunderts. Kirche mit sehr interessanten Festungsturm; eingefügt in einen sehr schönen Winkel, in dem sich auch die Kirche Vera-Cruz befindet.

SAN JUAN DE BARBALOS.
SAINT JEAN DE BARBALOS.
SAN JUAN DE BARBALOS.
SAN JUAN DE BARBALOS.

Iglesia románica del siglo XII.

Eglise romane du XIIᵉ siècle.

XIIth century Romanesque Church.

Romanische Kirche aus dem XII. Jahrhundert.

CASA DE SANTA TERESA.
MAISON DE STE. THERESE.
SANTA TERESA'S HOUSE.
HAUS DER SANTA TERESA.

Vivió la Santa en 1570.

La Sainte y vécut en 1570.

The Sain lived here in 1570.

Hier wohnte die Heilige im Jahre 1570.

SAN MARCOS. SAINT MAR.
SAN MARCOS. SAN MARCOS.

Interesante iglesia románica circular.

Eglise romane de forme circulaire.

Romanesque church in circular form.

Romanische Kirche, im Rundbau.

MUSEO UNIVERSITARIO.
MUSEE UNIVERSITAIRE.
UNIVERSITY MUSEUM.
UNIVERSITATSMUSEUM.

Patio de Escuelas (arqueología y pintura de los siglos XV y XVI).

Cour des Ecoles (archéologie et peintures du XVᵉ et XVIᵉ siècle).

Patio de Escuelas (archeology and paintings from the XV and XVI century).

Schulhof (Archäologie und Malerei aus dem 15. und 16. Jahrhundert).

MUSEO BIBLICO. MUSEE BIBLIQUE.
BIBLICAL MUSEUM. BIBLISCHES MUSEUM.
Paseo Canalejas, 87.

Teologado Padre Scio.

Teologado Padre Scio.

Teologado Padre Scio.

Theologische Fäkultat Padre Scio.

SALAMANCA DE NOCHE.
SALAMANQUE LA NUIT.
SALAMANCA AT NIGHT.
SALAMANCA BEI NACHT.

Los sábados, domingos y festivos, pueden admirarse los monumentos iluminados desde el anochecer hasta las doce de la noche en invierno y hasta la una de la madrugada en verano.

On peut admirer les monuments illuminés du coucher du soleil jusqu'à minuit en hiver et du coucher du soleil jusqu'à une heure du matin en été, les samedi, dimanche et fêtes.

On Saturdays, Sundays and holidays one can admire the illuminated monuments from nightfall until twelve during the winter and until one during the summer.

An Samstagen, Sonn-und Feiertagen kann man die beleuchteten Monumente von Einbruch der Dämmerung an bis um 24 h nachts im Winter und bis um 1 h morgens im Sommer bewundern.

Ciudad Rodrigo

LAS TRES COLUMNAS.
LES TROIS COLONNES.
THE THREE PILLARS.
DIE DREI SÄULEN.

Obras romanas, aunque se desconoce con certeza su procedencia y destino, son el blasón de la ciudad, con el significado que compendian los conocidos versos:

> Ciubdá-Rodrigo, en sennal
> de sus onrosas fortunas
> se zifra en tres colunas
> d'antigua, noble e leal.

Une oeuvre romaine dont on ignore exactement aussi bien l'origine que le destin. Ce sont les armoiries de la ville et ces quelques vers en résument la signification:

> Ciudad Rodrigo renferme
> Dans ses trois colonnes
> D'âge, de noblesse et de loyauté,
> Le blason de son honorable destinée.

Romanic work, even though their origin and destiny are not known they are the city's coat of arms with the significance which contracts the famous verses:

> Ciubdá-Rodrigo, en sennal
> de sus onrosas fortunas
> se zifra en tres colunas
> d'antigua, noble e leal.

Dieses Werk, geschaffen von der Römern —man weiss jedoch überhaupt nichts von der Herkunft noch Bestimmung der Säulen— sind das Symbol der Stadt; ihre Bedeutung wird in dem bekannten Vers umrissen:

> Ciubdá-Rodrigo, en sennal
> de sus onrosas fortunas
> se zifra en tres colunas
> d'antigua, noble e leal.

MURALLAS. *LES MURAILLES.*
WALLS. *STADTMAUERN.*

Posiblemente fue Fernando II quien decidió rodearla con una poderosa muralla, mandando llamar al gallego Juan de Cabrera para encomendarle las obras. Forma un óvalo irregular, de unos 2.250 metros, con muros almenados fabricados de cal y canto, con una altura de unos 13 metros y 2,10 metros de espesor, flanqueado por algunos torreones. También abrió varias puertas, conocidas con los nombres de: Puerta del Rey, de la Colada, de Santiago, de don Pelayo y del Conde, y, posteriormente, Puerta del Sol, del Alcázar y de la Santa Cruz. Fueron reparadas en distintas épocas con mampostería y en parte de sillería y tapial. En tiempo de Felipe V se rebajó su altura, a 7,55 metros y en 1710 fue reforzada nuevamente.

Hoy día están convertidas en un hermoso paseo que circunda toda la ciudad, y desde cuyos espléndidos miradores se contemplan bellísimos panoramas.

Ce fut très certainement Ferdinand II qui décida la construction d'une puissante muraille, autour de la ville. Il chargea des travaux le Galicien Juan de Cabrera. La muraille dessine un ovale irrégulier long de 2250 m crénelé, maçonné à chaux et à sable. Haute de 13 mètres, épaisse de 2,10 m elle est flanquée de quelques tours. On y perça aussi quelques portes connues sous les noms de: Puerta del Rey, de la Colada, de Santiago, de Don Pelayo et du Conde, plus tardivement les portes: del Sol, del Alcázar et de la Santa Cruz. A différentes époques elles furent réparées selon différents procédés: le limousinage ou les pierres de taille et le torchis. Sous le règne de Philippe V, on réduisit sa hauteur à 7,55 m et elle fut à nouveau consolidée en 1710.

C'est aujourd'hui une belle promenade qui fait le tour de la ville et d'où on peut admirer de merveilleux panoramas.

It was probably Fernando II who decided to surround it with a powerful wall, and he called for Juan de Cabrera from Galicia to entrust him with the job. It consists of an irregular oval, having a length of 2.250, with walls crowned with merlons manufactured with lime and blocks, with a height of 13 metres and a thickness of 2.10 meters, flanked by some round fortified towers. It also opened several doors, famous for names like: Puerta del Rey, de la Colada, de Santiago, de don Pelayo and del Conde, and de la Santa Cruz. They were repaired during different periods. With rubble-work and parts of the set of chairs and claymoulds. During Felipe V its height was lowered to 7.55 metres and in 1710 they are converted into a beautiful promenade which surrounds the whole town, and from its beautiful view-points you have beautiful panoramas.

Möglicherweise war es Fernando II, der beschlossen hate, die Stadt mit einer mächtigen Mauer zu umgeben und der den Galizier

Juan de Cabrera rufen liess, um ihn mit den Arbeiten zu beauftragen-Die Mauer bildet ein unregelmässiges Oval von ca. 2.250 m Länge, mit zinnenförmigen Wänden aus Kalk und Sand mit einer Höbe von ca. 13 m und 2,10 m Stärke und seitwarts einige Festungstürme gedeckt. Auch wurde sie mit verschiedenen Toren versehen, die unter den Namen Puerta del Rey, de la Colada, de Santiago, de don Pelayo, del Conde und die später erbaute Puerta del Sol, del Alcázar und de la Santa Cruz bekannt sind. Diese Tore wurden in verschiedenen Epochen mit Bruch- und teilweise Quadersteinen und Lehm ausgebessert. Zu Zeiten von Phillip V. wurde ihre Höhe auf 7,55 m herabgesetzt und 1710 auf's Neue verstärkt.

Heutzutage säumen sie eine wunderschöne Promenade rund um die ganze Stadt und von ihren prächtigen Aussichtstürmen aus geniesst man sehr schöne Panoramen.

EL CASTILLO DE ENRIQUE II DE TRASTAMARA.
LE CHÂTEAU DE HENRI II DE TRASTAMARE.
THE CASTLE OF ENRIQUE II DE TRASTAMARA.
SCHLOSS VON HEINRICH II VON TRASTAMARA.

Alcázar soberbio y antigua fortaleza de aspecto severo, muros almenados, con su barbacana y torre del homenaje. Enrique II de Trastamara se ocupó de construirlo, encomendándole las obras al arquitecto zamorano Lope Arias el año 1372, quien lo convirtió en un verdadero palacio-fortaleza. En la actualidad, tras diversas restauraciones, está convertido en Parador Nacional de la Subsecretaría de Turismo.

C'est un superbe château, une ancienne forteresse à l'aspect sévère, aux murs crênelés, dont on peut admirer le mâchicoulis et le donjon. Henri II le fit construire et chargea des travaux l'architecte Lope Arias, originaire de Zamora, en l'an 1372. Ce dernier en fit un véritable palais-forteresse. Après différentes restaurations, il est devenu de nos jours un Parador National du Secrétariat au Tourisme.

Superb castle and ancient fortress with a severs aspect, walls crowned with merlons, with its barbican and tower of homage. Enrique II de Trastamara was occupied to construct it, and sent for the architect Lope Arias from Zamora to do the job in the year 1372, who really converted it into a palace-fortress. Today, after several restaurations, it's converted into a National Halting Place of the Subsecretariate of Tourism.

Stolze Maurenburg und alte Festung mit ehrwürdigem Aussehen, zinnenförmigen Mauern, mit seiner Schiesscharte und Huldigungsturm. Heinrich II von. Trastamara beschäftigte sich mit ihrem Bau und übertrug die Arbeiten dem aus Zamora stammenden Architekten Lope Arias im Jahre 1372, der sie in einen wahrhaftigen Festungs-Palast wandelte. Nach verschiedenen Restaurationen ist sie heute ein nationaler Parador der Subsecretaria de Turismo.

IGLESIA CATEDRAL DE SANTA MARIA.
EGLISE CATHÉDRALE DE SAINTE MARIE.
CHURCH CATHEDRAL SANTA MARIA.
JUNGFRAU MARIA HAUPTKIRCHE.

Fundada por Fernando II, según privilegio del 17 de julio de 1165. Su planta basilical con tres naves, crucero y tres ábsides por cabecera, correspondiendo a las tres naves, tuvo por modelo la de Zamora. Empezada a finales del XII, la obra debió recibir su mayor impulso hacia el tercer decenio del XIII, acabándose prácticamente en el XIV. El claustro se comenzó también en este siglo, el ala del noroeste erigida por Benito Sánchez, cerrándose a partir de 1526 por mediación de Pedro de Güemes. La elegante capilla mayor fue reedificada en 1150, por Rodrigo Gil de Hontañón. La sillería del coro es obra de Rodrigo Alemán, asentada en 1498.

Fondée par Ferdinand II, selon le privilège de 17 juillet 1165, le plan de la Basilique comporte trois nefs, un transept et un chevet composé de trois absides, correspondant chacune d'elle à une nef. Elle fut construite sur le modèle de celle de Zamora. Les travaux, bien que commencés à la fin du XII° ne reçurent leur grande impulsion que dans la troisième décennie du XIII° siècle et ne prirent fin pratiquement qu'au XIV° siècle. Le cloître fut commencé à cette époque; Benito Sánchez édifia l'aile du nord-ouest et fut achevé à partir de 1526 sous la direction de Pedro de Güemes. La grande chapelle fut reconstruite en 1150 par Rodrigo Gil de Hontañón. Les chaises du choeur sont l'oeuvre de Rodrigo Alemán, elles furent installées en 1498.

It was founded by Fernando II as a privilege July 17, 1165. It's basilic floor with three naves transept, and three apses per upper end, corresponding to the three naves, had as model that of Zamora. It was started at the end of the XII century and the job got its most important impulse during the third decennium of the XIII century, and was practically finished in the XIV century. The gallery round the court was as well started during this century, the northwest wing was raised by Benito Sánchez, and was finished in 1526 by Rodrigo Gil de Hontañón. The set of chairs of the choir is a work of Rodrigo Alemán and was finished in 1498.

Gegründet von Ferdinand II. nach einem Sonderrecht vom 17. Juli 1165. Ihre Basilika mit drei Kirchenschiffen, Kreuzbogen und drei den Kirchenschiffen entsprechenden Wölbungen als Hauptteil, war der in Zamora stehenden Basilika nachgebaut worden. Am Ende des XII. Jahrhunderts begonnen, erhielt das Werk seinen grössten Antrieb im dritten Jahrzennt des XIII. Jahrhunderts und wurde praktisch im XIV beendet. Der Bau des Kreuzgangs wurde ebenfalls in diesem Jahrhundert begonnen und der von Benito Sánchez errichtete Nordwest-Flügel wurde ab 1526 durch Mitwirkung von Pedro de Güemes geschlossen. Die anmutige grössere Kapelle wurde 1150 durch Rodrigo Gil de Hontañón wiedererstellt. Das Chorgestühl ist das Werk von Rodrigo Alemán und wurde 1498 erstellt.

IGLESIA DE SAN PEDRO.
EGLISE SAINT PIERRE.
CHURCH SAN PEDRO.
HL. PETER KIRCHE.

Perteneciente al siglo XII, fue muy reedificada en el XVI, pero conserva un ábside de ladrillo de estilo mudéjar y una notable portada románica.

Elle appartient au XII° siècle mais elle a été reconstruite au XVI° siècle. Elle conserve une abside en brique de style «mudéjar» et un remarquable portail roman.

Belonging to the XII century, it was very much reconstructed during the XVI century, but it conserve an apse of brick in mohammedan style and a remarkable roman portal.

Aus dem XII. Jahrhundert stammend, wurde sie im XVI. Jahrhundert fast vollständig neuerrichtet, bewahrte jedoch ein Chorhaupt aus Backstein im Mudéjar-Stil und ein bemerkenswertes romanisches Portal.

IGLESIA DE SAN ANDRES.
EGLISE DE SAINT ANDRE.
CHURCH SAN ANDRES.
HL. ANDREAS KIRCHE.

Del templo románico subsisten las dos interesantísimas portadas.

Il ne subsiste du temple roman que deux interessants portails.

From the roman temple there are left two very interesting portals.

Aus den romanischen Zeiten stammen noch die zwei hochinteressanten Portale.

CONVENTO DE SAN FRANCISCO.
COUVENT DE SAINT FRANÇOIS.
MONASTERY SAN FRANCISCO.
HL. FRANZISKUS KLÖSTER.

Su fundación se atribuye al propio San Francisco, pero ya sólo quedan ruinas en lastimoso estado, que parecen corresponder a una reedificación en el siglo XVI.

On attribue sa fondation à Saint-François lui même, mais il n'en reste que de ruines navrantes datant selon toute vraisemblance d'une reconstruction du XVI° siècle.

It's foundation was attributed to San Francisco but now there are just ruins left in a pitiful shape, that seem to correspond to a reconstruction during the XVI century.

Seine Gründung wird dem Heiligen Franziskus selbst zugeschrieben; es existieren jedoch nur noch Ruinen in bedauernswertem Zustand, die darauf schliessen lassen, dass eine Wiedererrichtung im XVI. Jahrhundert durchgeführt wurde.

CONVENTO DE SAN AGUSTIN.
COUVENT DE SAINT AUGUSTIN.
MONASTERY SAN AGUSTIN.
HL. AUGUSTINUS KLÖSTER.

Fundado por Francisco de Chaves en 1483. Su iglesia es un buen edificio del siglo XVI.

Fondé par Francisco de Chaves en 1483. Son église est un bon monument du XVI° siècle.

Founded by Francisco de Chaves in 1483. It's church is a nice edifice from the XVI century.

Gegründet von Francisco de Chaves im Jahre 1483; seine Kirche ist ein schönes Bauwerk aus dem XVI. Jahrhundert.

CASA DE LOS CASTROS.
MAISON DE CASTRO.
THE HOUSE OF THE CASTROS.
CASA DE LOS CASTROS.

Fachada del siglo XVI, bien conservada salvo las dos torres primitivas, atribuida a Pedro de Güemes.

La façade date du XVI° siècle. Son état de conservation est bon exceptées les deux tours primitives qu'en attribue à Pedro de Güemes.

Façade from the XVI century, very well conserved except for the two primitive towers, atributed to Pedro de Güemes.

Fassade aus dem XVI. Jahrhundert, ausser den zwein primitiven Türmen gut erhalten und Werk von Pedro de Güemes.

CASA DE LOS AGUILAS.
MAISON DES AGUILAS.
THE HOUSE OF THE AGUILAS.
CASA DE LOS AGUILAS.

Hidalga mansión del siglo XVI, obra probable de Pedro de Güemes.

Manoir noble du XVIe siècle c'est certainement là encore une oeuvre de Pedro de Güemes.

A noble mansion from the XVI century, probably a work by Pedro de Güemes.

Herrschaftsgut aus dem XVI. Jahrhundert stammed und seor wahrscheinlich Werk von Pedro de Güemes.

CASA DE LA COLADA.
MAISON DE LA COLADA.
THE HOUSE OF THE COLADA.
CASA DE LA COLADA.

Se desconoce a qué familia perteneció, conservando detalles de exquisito gusto plateresco y una cadena, esculpida en piedra, símbolo de haber gozado del privilegio de asilo. También es atribuible al maestro Pedro de Güemes.

On ignore à quelle famille cette maison appartint, elle conserve des détails de style plateresque d'un goût exquis et une chaîne sculptée à même la pierre, symbole de sa qualité d'asile. On peut l'attribuer elle aussi au maître Pedro de Güemes.

It's not known to what family it belonged, conserving details of exquisite plateresque taste and a chain, sculptured in stone, symbol that it had the privilege of being a sanctuary. It's as well attributed to Pedro de Güemes.

Man weiss nicht, welcher Familie es gehörte; es bewahrt jedoch noch Einzelheiten erlesenen Geschmacks im Platereskenstil und ein in Stein gehauenes Rippengewölbe - ein Symbol, das ihm das Vorrecht einer Freistatte eiräumt. Auch dieses Werk stamm vom Meister Pedro de Güemes.

CASA DEL PRINCIPE.
MAISON DU PRINCE.
THE HOUSE OF THE PRINCE.
CASA DEL PRINCIPE.

Así llamada por haber sido palacio del Príncipe Mélito, don Iñigo de Mendoza. En su capilla se conserva un «Calvario» de Juan de Juni, procedente del convento de San Francisco.

Ainsi dénommée parce qu'elle fut un temps le palais du Prince Mélito, Iñigo de Mendoza.

Un calvaire de Juan de Juni, provenant du couvent de Saint François est conservé dans la chapelle.

It's called like this as it has been the Palace of Prince Mélito, don Iñigo de Mendoza. In its chapel is a «calvario» conserved of Juan de Juni, coming from the Monastery San Francisco.

So benannt, da es der Palast des Principe Mélito, don Iñigo de Mendoza, war. In der Kapelle existiert noch ein «Calvario» von Juan de Juni, das aus dem Hl. Franziskus Klöster stammt.

CASA AYUNTAMIENTO.
MAISON DE L'HÔTEL DE VILLE.
TOWN COUNCIL HOUSE.
RATHAUS.

Es del siglo XVI, con gracioso pórtico de arcos carpaneles sobre columnas en dos pisos. Una moderna restauración le ha hecho perder mucho carácter, desfigurando su aspecto.

Du XVIe siècle. Beau portique avec des arcs trilobés sur deux étages de colonnes. Une restauration récente lui a fait perdre de son caractère et, de ce fait, l'esthétique s'en trouve modifiée.

Belongs to the XVI century with a gracious portico of basket-handle arches on columns on two floors. Modern restauration has made it lose much of its character and has disfigured its vista.

Aus dem XVI. Jahrhundert mit zweistöckigem Säulengang. Durch die Einrichtung eines modernen Restaurants hat es viel von seinem Reiz verloren.

CAPILLA DEL CERRALBO.
CHAPELLE DE CERRALBO.
CHAPEL OF CERRALBO.
KAPELLE DES CERRALBO.

Fundada en el siglo XVI por el Cardenal don Francisco Pacheco y Toledo, arzobispo de Burgos, y antes Virrey de Nápoles. Es un monumento herreriano, eminentemente clásico, correcto y majestuoso.

Construite au XVIe siècle par le Cardinal Francisco Pacheco y Toledo, Archevêque de Burgos et, auparavant Vice-Roi de Naples. Du style d'Herrera, c'est un monument classique par excellence, bien conçu et majestueux.

Founded in the XVI century by Cardenal Francisco Pacheco y Toledo, the Archbishop of Burgos and former Viceroy of Naples. This is an eminently classical monument, correct and majestic.

Im XVI Jahrhundert gegründet, durch den Kardinal Francisco Pacheco und Toledo, Erzbischof von Burgos und zuvor Vizekönig von Napoles. Ein Heldenmonument klassischen Stils von grosser Majestät.

HOSPITAL DE LA PASION.
HÔPITAL DE LA PASSION.
HOSPITAL OF THE PASSION.
HOSPITAL DER PASSION.

Del siglo XVI, en cuya capilla se puede admirar un maravilloso «Calvario» fechado en 1563, de estilo italiano.

Du XVIe siècle; on peut admirer dans la chapelle un très beau «Calvaire» de style italien et qui remonte à l'année 1563.

Belonging to the XVI century, in whose chapel a wonderful «Calvary» dated in 1563, in Italian style, may be admired.

Aus dem XVI. Jahrhundert, in der Kapelle kann man einen herrlichen Leidensweg aus dem Jahre 1563 italienischen Stils betrachten.

1.2. BIBLIOTECAS
BIBLIOTHEQUES
LIBRARIES
BIBLIOTHEKEN

BIBLIOTECA POPULAR. Generalísimo, 24.
BIBLIOTECA GENERAL DE LA UNIVERSIDAD. Edificio de la Universidad.
BIBLIOTECAS ESPECIALIZADAS EN LAS FACULTADES DE LETRAS, CIENCIAS, DERECHO Y MEDICINA.
BIBLIOTECA DE LA CAJA DE AHORROS. Pasaje, 2.
ATENEO DE SALAMANCA. Gran Vía, 11, 2.º. (Sala de exposiciones, bibliotecas, seminarios de cine, teatro, agrupación fotográfica, club de letras, peña ajedrecista).

1.3. ARTESANIA
ARTISANAT
GRAFTWORK
KUNSTHANDWERK

La provincia es una de las áreas más ricas del arte popular europeo (piel, madera, hueso, tejidos, metales, mimbre, bordados, etcétera). Se encuentran ricamente adornados todos los variados objetos de uso diario.
Exposición y venta: «Artesanía» (Edificio de la Delegación Provincial de Sindicatos). Gran Vía, 55. Igual horario que el comercio. Sábados por la tarde, cerrado.

La province de Salamanque est une des contrées les plus riches en art populaire européen (peaux, bois, os, tissus, métaux, osier, broderies, etc...). Les objects d'usage quotidien sont eux aussi richement décorés.

Exposition et vente: *«Artesanía» (bâtiment de la délégation provinciale des syndicats.) Gran Vía 55. Aux mêmes heures que les établissements de commerce. Fermé le samedi après-midi.*

The province is one of the richest areas in popular European art (leather, wood, bone weaving, metal, willow-twig, embroidery, etc). You find all kinds of richly decorated things for daily use.
Exposition and Sale: «Crafts» (Edificio de la Delegación Provincial de Sindicatos). Gran Vía, 55. The same timetable as the shops. Saturday afternoons, closed.

*Die Provinz ist eine der an volkstümlicher europäischer Kunst reichsten Gegenden (Leder, Holz, Knochen, Textilien, Metalle, Korbwaren, Stickereien, usw.) Die verschiedensten Gegenstände des täglichen Gebrauchs sind reich verziert.
Ausstellung und Verkauf: «Kunsthandwerk» (Edificio de la Delegación Provincial de Sindicatos), Gran Vía, 55. Geschäftsarbeitszeit. An Samstagen abends geschlossen.*

1.4. ALFARERIA
POTERIE
THE ART OF THE POTTER
TÖPFERARBEITEN

ANIANO PEREZ. Travesía del Norte, 6 (Alba de Tormes).
SANTIAGO PEREZ DOMINGUEZ. (Alba de Tormes.)
TADEO PEREZ. (Alba de Tormes.)

1.5. BORDADOS TIPICOS
BRODERIES TYPIQUES
TYPICAL EMBROIDERY
TYPISCHE STICKEREIEN

ELISA MERCHAN MANCEBO. (La Alberca.)
SUCESO PEREZ HERNANDEZ. (Fuente de San Esteban.)

1.6. BOTOS CAMPEROS
BOTTES DE CHEVAL RUSTIQUES
A ROUGH WINE SKIN
ANDALUSISCHE LANDSTIEFEL

VICTORIANO GONZALEZ HERRERO. Plaza del Corrillo, 3. Salamanca.
MELCHOR IZQUIERDO SANCHEZ. (Macotera.)
EZEQUIEL SALGADO GOMEZ. (Carrascal del Obispo.)

1.7. CENCERROS
SONNAILLES
BELLS WORN BY CATTLE
VIEHSCHELLEN

FRANCISCO GARCIA TABARES. (Ciudad Rodrigo.)

1.8. **ESMALTES DE ARTE**
  EMAUX
  ENAMEL WORK
  KUNSTARBEITEN IN EMAILLE

LUIS GARCIA HUERTA. Rúa Mayor, 35. Salamanca.

1.9. **FABRICACION DE ROMANAS**
  FABRICATION DE PESONS
  MANUFACTURE OF WRIGHTS
  HERSTELLUNG VON SCHNELLWAAGEN

ANGEL GARZON APARICIO. Rúa del Sol, 25 (Ciudad Rodrigo).

1.10. **FILIGRANA CHARRA**
  FILIGRANE «CHARRA»
  SPUN WORK
  RUSTIKALE FILIGRANARBEITEN

JOSE CORDON DE BLAS. San Pablo, 1. Salamanca.
VASCONCELLOS, S. A. Juan Arias, 25. (Ciudad Rodrigo.)

1.11. **HIERROS FORJADOS**
  FER FORGE
  FORGED IRON
  SCHMIEDEEISEN

ANTONIO BORREGO. (Aldehuela de la Bóveda.)
PALACIO DEL HIERRO. San Pablo, 56. Salamanca.

1.12. **IMAGINERIA DE ARTE ANTIGUO: CE-**
  RAMICA
  STATUETTES D'ART ANCIEN: CERA-
  MIQUES
  ANTIQUE ART: CERAMICS
  PHANTASIEARBEITEN   ANTIQUER
  KUNST: KERAMIKEN

GERARDO SANCHEZ CRUZ. Doyagüe, 3. Salamanca.

1.13. **MUEBLES ESTILO ESPAÑOL**
  MEUBLES DE STYLE ESPAGNOL
  SPANISH STYLE FURNITURE
  MEUBLES DE STYLE SPAGNOL

CARLOS HERNANDEZ. San Gregorio, 7. Salamanca.

1.14. **MUEBLES DE MIMBRE**
  MEUBLE EN OSIER
  WILLOW-TWIG FURNITURE
  KORBEMÖBEL

GONZALO CORTES. (Villoruela.)

1.15. **MUÑEQUERIA DE FIELTRO**
  POUPÉES EN FEUTRE
  FELT DOLLS
  SPIELZEUG AUS FILZ

HERMANAS ALMEIDA. Bermejeros, 52. Salamanca.

1.16. **TEJIDOS**
  TISSUS
  WEAVING
  TEXTILIEN

ANTONIO SANCHEZ ABALLOS. Pozo, 10. (Macotera.)

2. ALOJAMIENTOS LOGEMENTS ACCOMMODATION UNTERKÜNFTE

2.1. **HOTELES**
  HOTELS
  HOTELS
  HOTELS

Categoria 4 Estrellas. Categorie 4 Étoiles.
4 Star Category. Kategorie 4 Sterne.

Salamanca

GRAN HOTEL. Plaza Poeta Iglesia, 3.
MONTERREY. J. A. Primo de Rivera, 13.
REGIO. Carretera Villacastin a Vigo Km. 204.

Categoria 3 Estrellas. Categorie 3 Étoiles.
3 Star Category. Kategorie 3 Sterne.

Salamanca

ALFONSO X. Generalisimo Franco, 48.
EL ZAGUAN. Ruiz Aguilera, 3.

Béjar

COLON. Afueras Santa Ana, s/n.

Ciudad Rodrigo

PARADOR NACIONAL. Castillo Enrique II.

Ledesma

VEGA DE TIRADOS.
BALNEARIO DE LEDESMA.

Categoria 2 Estrellas. Categorie 2 Étoiles.
2 Star Category. Kategorie 2 Sterne.

Salamanca

PASAJE. Espoz y Mina, 11.
CONDAL. Plaza Hnos. Jerez, 2.
MILAN. Plaza del Angel, 6.
TORIO. Avda. Mirat, 13.
MINDANAO. Avda: Líbano, 2.
LAGUNA. Consuelo, 13.
CARABELA. Plaza de España, 3.
CEYLAN. Plaza Peso, 10.
EMPERATRIZ. Compañia, 4.
EL QUINTO PINO. Carret. Valladolid, Km. 231.
URIA. Garcia Moreno, 1.
ALIANZA II. Plaza Carmelitas.
ARAGON. Avda. Federico Anaya, 1.
CONDE DAVID Avda de Italia, 48
GABRIEL Y GALAN. Plaza Grabiel y Galán, 1.
INTERNACIONAL. Avda. Mirat, 13.
LOS CHARROS. Pollo Martín, 10.
ORIENTAL. José Antonio, 7.

Alba de Tormes

BENEDICTINO. Benitas, 6.

Béjar

BLAZQUEZ SANCHEZ. Trav. Santa Ana.

Candelario

CRISTI. Simón López, 14.

La Alberca

LAS BATUECAS. Fuente canal.

Ledesma

BALNEARIO (de 1-VI a 30-IX).

Martinamor

CUATRO CALZADAS. Carret. Gijón-Sevilla, Km. 17.

2.2. ACAMPAMENTOS TURISTICOS
   CAMPINGS
   CAMPINGS SITES
   ZELTPLÄTZE

CABRERIZOS «Don Quijote». Km. 3 de Aldealuenga a Salamanca. 1.ª categoría.
SANTA MARTA DE TORMES. «Regio». Km. 204. Ctra. Villacastín-Vigo. 1.ª categoría.

3. GASTRONOMIA
   GASTRONOMIE
   GASTRONOMY
   GASTRONOMIE

3.1. RESTAURANTES
   RESTAURANTS
   RESTAURANTS
   RESTAURANTS

**4 Tenedores. 4 Fourchettes.
4 Fork category. 4 Gabeln.**

Salamanca

COMPLEJO TURISTICO «LAS TORRES». Carretera Madrid, Km. 2.
FEUDAL. Plaza poeta Iglesias, 3.
MESON LAZARILLO DE TORMES. 4 Km., carretera de Madrid.

**3 Tenedores. 3 Fourchettes.
3 Fork category. 3 Gabeln.**

EL CANDIL. Plaza de la Reina, 2.
VENECIA. Plaza del Mercado, 2.

3.2. ESPECIALIDADES GASTRONOMICAS
   SPECIALITES GASTRONOMIQUES
   GASTRONOMIC SPECIALITIES
   SPEZIALITATEN

SALAMANCA: «Chanfaina» (arroz con menudos de ave, cordero y chorizo). Confiteria: los típicos «chochos» y el «bollo maimón».
ALBA DE TORMES: «Almendras de Santa Teresa» (garapiñadas).
BEJAR: el tradicional «calderillo» (guiso de carne y patatas a fuego lento, en la típica caldera).
CIUDAD RODRIGO: Huevos fritos con «farinato» (embutido caracteristico).
GUIJUELO: Jamón y embutidos.
PEÑARANDA DE BRACAMONTE: Asado de cochinillo «tostón» y de cabrito.
En toda la provincia, con ocasión de fiestas, el «hornazo» (empanada a base de embutidos y jamón), tostón, etc.
SALAMANQUE: «Chanfaina» (riz condimenté avec des abats de volaille, de l'agneau et du chorizo). En confiserie on trouve les célèbres «chochos» et le «bollo maimón».

ALBA DE TORMES: Les pralines de Sainte Thérèse.

BEJAR: Le traditional «calderillo» (ragoût de viande et de pommes de terre préparé à feu doux dans le typique chaudron).

CIUDAD RODRIGO: Les oeufs frits avec du «farinato» (charcuterie caractéristique).

GUIJUELO: Jambon et diverses charcuteries.

PEÑARANDA DE BRACAMONTE: «Le Tostón» (cochon de lait rôti) et chevreau.

A l'occasion des fêtes on trouve dans toute la province «l'Hornazo» (genre de grand chausson à base de jambon et diverse charcuterie), le tostón, etc...

SALAMANCA: «Chanfaina» (rice with pieces of poultry, lamb or salami). Confectionary: the typical «chochos» and the «bollo maimón».

ALBA DE TORMES: «Almendras (almonds) de Santa Teresa (sugar coated).»

BEJAR: The traditional «calderillo» (meat and potato stew cooked on a slow flame, in the typical «caldera» (boiler).

CIUDAD RODRIGO: Fried eggs with «farinato» (typical sausage).

GUIJUELO: Ham and sausages.

PEÑARANDA DE BRACAMONTE: Roast suckling pig «tostón» and kid.

In the entire province, during fiestas, the «hornazo» (meat pie made of sausages and ham), suckling pig, etc.

SALAMANCA: «Chanfaina» (Reis mit Geflügelklein, Lamm und chorizo); Süsswaren; die typischen «chochos» und der «bollo maimón».

ALBA DE TORMES: «Almendras de Santa Teresa» (kandiert).

BEJAR: Das traditionelle «calderillo»(Fleischgericht mit Kartoffeln, auf schwachem Feuer zubereitet, im typischen Kessel).

CIUDAD RODRIGO: Spiegeleier mit «farinato» (charakteristische Wurstwaren).

GUIJUELO: Schinken und Wurstwaren.

PEÑARANDA DE BRACAMONTE: Braten vom Jungschwein «tostón» und Zicklein.

Überall in der Provinz wird an Festtagen der «hornazo» (Fleischgebäck bestehend aus Wurstwaren und Schinken) und «tostón» serviert.

**Vinos. Vins.
Wine. Wein.**

Vino tinto serrano y clarete de la Ribera.

Vin rouge «serrano», et vin rosé de la Ribera.

Red highland wine and Ribera claret.

Rotwein «serrano» und blassroter Ribera-Wein.

4. AGENDA PRACTICA
AGENDA PRATIQUE
PRACTICAL AGENDA
PRAKTISCHES NACHSCHLA-
GEWERK

4.1 CONSULADOS
CONSULATS
CONSULATES
KONSULEN

FRANCIA. Generalísimo Franco, 21.
ITALIA. Calvo Sotelo, 4, 3.º-D.
PORTUGAL. Doctor Piñuela, 2, 3.º.
PERU. Gran Capitán, 6.
SUECIA. Bordadores, 6.

4.2. DIRECCIONES Y SERVICIOS UTILES
ADRESSES ET SERVICES UTILES
USEFUL ADDRESSES AND SERVICES
NOTZLICHE ADRESSEN UND DIENSTE

**Correos, telegrafos y teléfonos.
Télégraphes et téléphones.
Post and telegraph office and telephone exchange.
Post-und Telegraphenamt.**

**Correos. Postes.
Post Offices. Postämter.**

CORREOS. Plaza de Hermanos Jerez, 1.
TELEGRAFOS. En el mismo edificio que Correos.
TELEFONOS. Plaza de los Bandos. Información: 003. Conferencias: 009. Torres Villarroel, 34.

**Teléfonos de urgencia
Téléphones d'urgence
Emergency telephone numbers
Notrute**

AMBULANCIA NUESTRA SEÑORA DE LA MERCED. Gran Vía, 27. Telf. 21 20 47.
AMBULANCIA CRUZ ROJA. Plaza de San Benito. Telf. 21 56 42.
SERVICIO MEDICO DE URGENCIA. RESIDENCIA VIRGEN DE LA VEGA. Paseo de San Vicente. Telf. 21 87 02-3-4-5.
JEFATURA NACIONAL DE SANIDAD. Valencia, 12. Telf. 22 02 84.
GUARDIA CIVIL DE TRAFICO. Plaza de Colón. Telf. 21 98 60.
HOSPITAL PROVINCIAL. García Tejada, 3. Telf. 21 51 03-4.
HOSPITAL SANTISIMA TRINIDAD. Avda. Alemania, 48 Telf. 21 80 00 y 21 97 87.
CASA DE SOCORRO. Nueva de San Bernardo, 2. Telf. 21 99 99.
BOMBEROS. Avda. Campoamor. Telf. 21 45 45.

Comunicaciones (Autobuses)
Communications (Autobus)
Communications (Buses)
Verkehrsverbindungen (Buslinien)

SALAMANCA-ALBA DE TORMES. 21 Km. Plaza del Campillo, 1.
SALAMANCA-BEJAR. 72 Km. Valencia, 28.
SALAMANCA-CACERES (y Plasencia). 214 Km. Rector Esperabé, 21.
SALAMANCA-CIUDAD RODRIGO. 88 Km. Plaza San Isidro.
SALAMANCA-LA ALBERCA. 76 Km. Plaza San Isidro.
SALAMANCA-LEDESMA. 34 Km. Valencia, 28.
SALAMANCA-TORO (Zamora). 75 Km. Mercado de San Juan.
SALAMANCA-MADRID (por Avila y Arévalo). 200 y 223 Km. respectivamente. Rúa Antigua, 9.
SALAMANCA-ZAMORA. 64 Km. Mercado de San Juan.
SALAMANCA-VALLADOLID-LEON. 114 y 247 Km., respectivamente. Juan Picornel, 7. (Garaje Nuño).
SALAMANCA-SEVILLA. 483 Km. Plaza España (Cafetería Niágara).

Estaciones de Servicio
Stations Service
Petrol Stations
Tankstellen mit Service

SALAMANCA. Carretera Villacastín-Vigo, Km. 209,4.
SALAMANCA. Avda. de Mirat, 18.
SALAMANCA. Carretera Salamanca-Cáceres, Km. 1,9.
SALAMANCA. Carretera Gijón-Sevillla, Km. 213,5.
SALAMANCA. Carretera Burgos-Portugal, Km. 233,3.
SALAMANCA (Tejares). Carretera Burgos-Fuentes de Oñoro, Km. 240,8.
ALBA DE TORMES. Carretera Alba de Tormes-Piedrahita, Km. 0,450.
BEJAR. Carretera Salamanca-Béjar, Km. 72,5.
CALVARRASA DE ABAJO. Carretera Madrid-Salamanca, km. 199,7.
CALZADA DE DON DIEGO. Carretera Burgos-Portugal, Km. 256,4.
CAMPO DE PEÑARANDA. Carretera Peñaranda-Campo Peñaranda. Km. 26,4.
CIUDAD RODRIGO. Carretera Burgos-Salamanca, Km. 322,9.
ENCINAS DE ABAJO. Carretera Madrid-Salamanca, Km. 113,2.
FRESNO-ALHANDIGA. Carretera Salamanca-Sevilla, Km. 30,4.
FUENTE DE SAN ESTEBAN. Carretera Burgos-Salamanca, Km. 289,2.

FUENTES DE OÑORO. Carretera Burgos-Salamanca, Km. 349,7.
GUIJUELO. Carretera Salamanca-Cáceres, Km. 47,5.
LEDESMA. Carretera Salamanca-Fermoselle, Km. 1,3.
MACOTERA. Carretera Piedrahita-Medina, Km. 48,7.
PEÑARANDA DE BRACAMONTE. Carretera Cañizal-Piedrahita, Km. 38,2.
RAGAMA. Carretera Medina-Peñaranda, Km. 40,4.
SANTA MARTA DE TORMES. Carretera Salamanca-Alba de Tormes, Km. 1,1.
TAMAMES. Carretera Seperos-Fermoselle, Km. 51,3.
VALDECARROS. Carretera Macotera-Anaya de Alba, Km. 24,9.
VILLAFLORES. Carretera Villaflores-Cantalapiedra, Km. 28,2.
VILLARES DE LA REINA. Carretera Burgos-Salamanca, Km. 231,8.
VILLAVIEJA DE YELTES. Carretera SA-322 a N-620, Km. 18,7.
VITIGUDINO. Carretera Salamanca-Portugal, Km. 67,7.

Talleres de reparación de automóviles. (Agencias oficiales)
Ateliers de reparation d'automobiles. (Agences Officielles)
Car repair garages. (Oficial Agencies)
Autoreparaturwerkstantten. (Offizielle Agenturen)

ARGOS. Zamora, 30. (Ford, Alfa Romeo y Perkins.)
AUTO HERNANDEZ. Batuecas, 2 y 4 (Barrio Salas Pombo). Avda. Portugal, 48. (DKW).
AUTO-SALAMANCA, S. A. Torres Villarroel, 37. (Renault).
BALMASA, S. A. Torres Villarroel, 4. (Land Rover, Rover, Morris, MG, Commer, Singer, Hilman, Sunbeam, Humber, Grupos BMC y Rooter).
EL MOTOR NACIONAL, S. A. Avda. Portugal, 78. (Simca y Dodge).
MARTIN JIMENEZ. Carretera Valladolid, Km. 2. (Sava-Austin).
MONEO, S. A. Ramon y Cajal, 17. (Seat, Fiat y Moto Vespa).
MUÑO. Avda. Italia, 3 y 5 (Palacio del Automóvil). Avda. de Italia, 4 (Garaje Monumental). Avda. Mirat, 29. (Seat, Austin, Peugeot, Mercedes, Volkswagen, Land-Rover, Borgward y Skoda).
VICENTE SANCHEZ MARCOS. Avda. Mirat, 19. Los Zúñiga, 7. (Citroën).
VIHER. Fray Luis de Granada, 5. (Fiat, Seat y Simca).

5. FIESTAS Y ESPECTACULOS FÊTES ET SPECTACLES FESTIVITIES AND SPECTACLES FESTE UND SCHAUSPIELE

5.1. CLUBS Y SOCIEDADES DEPORTIVAS CLUBS ET SOCIETES SPORTIVES CLUBS AND SPORTS SOCIETIES CLUBS UND SPORTCLUBS

REAL AUTOMOVIL CLUB DE ESPAÑA. Gran Vía, 6. Telf. 21 29 25.
AUTOMOVIL CLUB DE SALAMANCA. Frutos Valiente, 2. Dep. 15. Telf. 22 02 95.
CAMPO DE TIRO Y DEPORTES. Carretera de Madrid. Telf. 21 20 22. Oficinas: Arriba, 21. Telf. 21 42 33.
ASOCIACION DE CAZADORES Y PESCADORES. Arriba, 21. Telf. 21 26 75.
UNION DEPORTIVA SALAMANCA. Avda. General Mola, 1. Telf. 22 20 90.
HIPICA DE SALAMANCA. Carretera de Madrid (en el Campo de Tiro y Deportes). Telf. 21 20 22.
PISCINA CLUB REGIO. Carretera de Madrid (N-501). Km. 204,7.
PISCINA CAMPO DE TIRO Y DEPORTES. Carretera de Madrid.
PISCINA INFANTIL. Parque General Primo de Rivera (Alamedilla).
COMPLEJO «LAS TORRES». Carretera de Madrid.
PLAYAS FLUVIALES. Puente del Congosto. Santa Marta de Tormes, Ledesma y Alba de Tormes.
CLUB NAUTICO. Pantano de Santa Teresa.
INSTALACIONES DEPORTIVAS DEL CAMPO DE TIRO Y DEPORTES. Carretera de Madrid (Tenis, tiro, hípica, piscina, etc.).
CAMPO DE FUTBOL.
GIMNASIO UNIVERSITARIO. (Recinto Universitario).
PABELLON MUNICIPAL DE DEPORTES «OTERO AENLLE». Parque Alamedilla (Baloncesto, tenis, boxeo, patinaje, hockey).
PARQUE INFATIL DE TRAFICO. Parque Alamedilla (Juegos, piscinas).
MONTAÑISMO. En las sierras de Béjar, Peña de Francia y Ciudad Rodrigo.
DEPORTES DE NIEVE. Sierra de Béjar.

5.2. CAZA Y PESCA CHASSE ET PÊCHE HUNTING AND FISHING JAGD UND FISCHFANG

Caza Mayor
Gros gibier
Big game hunting
Grosswild

Jabalí: Frecuente en el SO. del partido de Béjar. Abundante en el sur del partido de Ciudad Rodrigo y SO. del partido de Sequeros.
Zorro: Frecuente en los partidos de Ciudad Rodrigo, Vitigudino y Sequeros. Abundante en el partido de Ledesma.

Sanglier: *Fréquent au sud-ouest du territoire de Béjar, il est abondant au sud du territoire de Ciudad Rodrigo, et au sud-ouest du territoire de Sequeros.*
Renard: *Fréquent sur le territoire de Ciudad Rodrigo, de Vitigudino et de Sequeros. Il est abondant sur le territoire de Ledesma.*

Wild boar: Frequent in the southwest of Béjar. Abundant in the south part of Ciudad Rodrigo and in the southwest of the part Sequeros.
Fox: Frequent in the parts of Ciudad Rodrigo, Vitigudino and Sequeros. Abundant in the part of Ledesma.

Wildeschewein: *kommt häufig vor im Südwestendes Bezirks Béjar und reichlich vorhanden im Süden des Bezirks Ciudad Rodrigo und im Südwesten von Sequeros.*
Fuchs: *kommt häufig vor im Raum Ciudad Rodrigo, Vitigudino und Sequeros. Besonders häufig im Bezirk Ledesma.*

Caza Menor
Menu gibier
Hunting
Kleinwild

Aves acuáticas: Frecuentes en el partido de Alba de Tormes.
Paloma: Frecuente en los partidos de Sequeros, sur del partido de Salamanca y en el partido de Vitigudino. Abundante en los de Ledesma y Ciudad Rodrigo.
Perdiz: Frecuente en los partidos de Vitigudino, Ledesma, Peñaranda, Ciudad Rodrigo, Béjar y sur del partido de Salamanca. Abundante en el norte y centro del partido de Salamanca y en los partidos de Alba de Tormes y Sequeros. Muy abundante en el sur del partido de Sequeros.
Conejo: Frecuente en el partido de Sequeros.
Liebre: Frecuente en los partidos de Alba de Tormes, Peñaranda y Salamanca.

Oiseaux aquatiques: *Ils sont fréquents sur le territoire d'Alba de Tormes.*
Pigeons: *Fréquents sur le territoire de Sequeros, au sud du territoire de Salamanque et sur le territoire de Vitigudino, il est abondant sur les territoires de Ledesma et Ciudad Rodrigo.*
Perdrix: *Fréquents sur les territoires de Vitigudino, Ledesma, Peñaranda, Ciudad Rodrigo, Béjar et au sud du territoire de Salamanque, elle est abondante au nord et au centre du territoire de Salamanque et sur le territoire*

d'Alba de Tormes et Sequeros. Très abondante au sud du territoire de Sequeros.
Lapin: Fréquents sur le territoire de Sequeros.
Lièvre: Fréquent sur le territoire d'Alba de Tormes, de Peñaranda et de Salamanque.

Water fowl: Frequent in the parts of Alba de Tormes.
Dove: Frequent in the parts of Sequeros, south of the part of Salamanca and in the part of Vitigudino. Abundant in the parts of Ledesma and Ciudad Rodrigo.
Partridge: Frequent in the parts of Vitigudino, Ledesma, Peñaranda, Ciudad Rodrigo, Béjar and south of the part of Salamanca. Abundant in the north and central parts of Salamanca and in the parts of Alba de Tormes and Sequeros. Very abundant in the south of the part of Sequeros.
Rabbit: Frequent in the parts of Sequeros.
Hare: Frequent in the parts of Alba de Tormes, Peñaranda and Salamanca.

Wasservogel: kommen häufig vor im Raum Alba de Tormes.
Tauben: kommen häufig vo in den Bezirken von Sequeros, im Süden von Salamanca und im Raum Vitigudino. Besonders reichlich vorhanden im Bezirk Ledesma und Ciudad Rodrigo.
Rebhuhn: kommen häufig vor im Raum Vitigudino, Ledesma, Peñaranda, Ciudad Rodrigo, Béjar, und im Süden des Bezirks Salamanca. Besonders reichlich vorhanden im Norden und im Zentrum des Raumes Salamanca und in den Bezirken von Alba de Tormes und Sequeros. Überreichlich im Süden von Sequeros.
Kaninchen: kommen häufig vor im Bezirk Sequeros.
Hasen: kommen häufig vor im Raum von Alba de Tormes, Peñaranda und Salamanca.

Pesca.
Pêche.
Fishing
Fischfang

Especies: Truchas, barbos, carpas, percas, cangrejos.
Ríos: Tormes, Francia, Frío, Olleros o Mayas, Alagón, Cuerpo de Hombre, Duero, Agueda y Yeltes.
Pantanos: De Santa Teresa, Villagonzalo (río Tormes). De Aldeadávila y Saucelle (río Duero). Embalse del Agueda (Ciudad Rodrigo).
Cotos: Aldeadávila (cangrejos), Alba de Tormes, Galisancho, Río Francia, Río Frío, Río Olleros (truchas).

Espèces: Truites, barbeaux, carpes, tanches, écrevisses.

Rivières: Le Tormes, le Francia, l'Olleros ou Mayas, le Frío, l'Alagón, le Cuerpo de Hombre, le Douro, l'Agueda et le Yeltes.
Retenues d'eau: Celles de Santa Teresa, de Villagonzalo (río Tormes), d'Aldeadávila, et Saucelle (rio Douro), de l'Agueda (Ciudad Rodrigo).
Pêche gardée: Aldeadávila (écrevisses), Alba de Tormes, Galisancho, Rio Francia, Río Frío, Río Olleros (truites).

Types of fish: Trout, barbel, carpp, tench, crayfish.
Rivers: Tormes, Francia, Frío, Olleros o Mayas, Alagón, Cuerpo de Hombre, Duero, Agueda and Yeltes.
Artificial lakes: De Santa Teresa, Villagonzalo (río Tormes). De Aldeadávila y Saucelle (Río Duero). Embalse del Agueda (Ciudad Rodrigo).
Breeding grounds: Aldeadávila (crayfish), Alba de Tormes, Galisancho, Río Francia, Río Frío, Río Olleros (trouts).

Arten: Forellen, Barben, Karpfen, Schleien, Flusskrebse.
Flüsse: Tormes, Francia, Frio, Olleros oder Mayas, Alagón, Cuerpo de Hombre, Duero, Agueda und Yeltes.
Stauseen: Santa Teresa, Villagonzalo (Tormes), Aldeadávila und Saucelle (Duero), Stausee del Agueda (Ciudad Rodrigo).
Jagdgehege: Aldeadávila (Flusskrebse), Alba de Tormes, Galisancho, Río Francia, Rio Frío, Río Olleros (Forellen).

5.3. ESPECTACULOS
SPECTACLES
SHOWS
SCHAUSPIELE

Salas de fiestas. Cabarets.
Night clubs. Tanzlokale.

ATENAS. Avd. General Mola, 1.
ALTAMIRA. Plaza Mayor, 35.
CASINO DE SALAMANCA. Zamora, 3.
CLUB 21. Gran Hotel.
CUEVA DE LA MUCHERES. Recinto Feria Monográfica. Paseo del Campo Charro.
DANIEL'S WHISKY CLUB. Gran Vía, 4.
EL CABALLO BLANCO. Plaza Hermanos Jerez, 2.
JOCKEY. Calvo Sotelo, 1.
LAS TORRES. Carretera de Madrid, Km. 2.
NIGHT CLUB EDEN. Gran Vía, 20.
OXFORD. Pasaje José Antonio.
PARRILLA MONTERREY. Hotel Monterrey.
RUA CLUB. Rúa, 42.
CLUB ORIENTAL. Dimas Madariaga, 2.
CLUB LOS FAROLES. Hovohambre, 2.
COMPLEJO TURISTICO LAS TORRES. Ctra. Madrid a 2 Km.

EL CORZO. Calvo Sotelo, 3.
EL MESON DEL MARQUES. Plaza de Es-
paña, 3.
EL MESON DE SANCHO PANZA. Cuesta de la
Raqueta, 6.
EL ZAGUAN. Ruiz Aguilera, 3.
ESPAÑA. Plaza de España, 1.
FERIA MONOGRAFICA. Avda. Campo Charro.
FONTANA. Gran Vía, 2.
GO-GO STREET. Plaza de España, 1.
LA CAMELIA. Clavel, 9.
LA POSADA. Aire, 1.
LIDO. Avda. de Portugal, 44.
LORCA CLUB. Gran Vía, 13.
LOS NARDOS. Plaza Hermanos Jerez, 2.
MORRISON. Zamora, 1.
NEGURI. Avda. de Mirat, 4.
NUEVA YORK CLUB. Gran Vía, 4.
PACIFICO. Plaza del Ejército, 4.
PLUS ULTRA. Concejo, 2.
ROMA. Ruiz Aguilera, 8.
WHISKY ROOM. Gran Vía, 2.
ZOSKA. Calvo Sotelo, 1.

Plaza de toros
Arenes. Bullrings.
Stierkampfarenas.

PLAZA DE TOROS. Carretera de Valladolid.
Monumento Nacional al Toro de Lidia.
PEÑA TAURINA. Bar la Goleta. Van Dyck, 21.

Tientas turísticas.
Tientas touristiques.
Tourist Bullfighting.
Turistische stierkampfveranstaltungen.

FINCA RODASVIEJAS. Término de Aldehuela
de la Bóveda, carretera N-620, de Salamanca
a Ciudad Rodrigo, a 35 Km. de Salamanca,
(plaza de tientas, ganadería brava, capeas,
festivales, restaurantes, cafetería, aparca-
miento, alquiler de caballo, etc.).
LA CAPEA. En Chamberí (Salamanca), a 1 Km.
de la capital. Escuela taurina, plaza de tientas.

PROPRIETE «RODASVIEJAS». Municipalité de
Aldehuela de la Bóveda, route nationale 620
allant de Salamanque à Ciudad Rodrigo, à 35
km. de Salamanque. (Arènes de tientas,
taureaux bravos, «capeas», festivals, restau-
rant, cafétéria, parking, location de chevaux,
etc...)
PROPRIETE «LA CAPEA» à Chamberi (Sala-
manque), à un kilomètre de la capitale.
(Ecole taurine, arènes de tientas.)

FINCA RODASVIEJAS. End of Aldehuela de la
Bóveda, highway N-620, from Salamanca to
Ciudad Rodrigo, at a distance of 35 km from
Salamanca, (the bullfighting ring, excellent

cattle-ranch, amateur bullfights with a calf
that is not killed, festivals, restaurants, cafe-
terías, parkings places, hiring of horses, etc.).

LA CAPEA: At Chamberi (Salamanca) at 1 km
from the town. Bullfigying school, bullfight
ring for tourists.

FINCA RODASVIEJAS. Am Ende der Aldehuela
de la Bóveda gelegen, carretera N-620, auf
der Strecke von Salamanca nach Ciudad Ro-
drigo, 35 km von Salamanca entfernt, (plaza
de tientas, Wildviehzucht, Amateurkämpfe mit
Jungstieren, Festivals, Restaurants, Cafés,
Parkplatz, Pferdeverleih, usw.).

LA CAPEA. In Chamberi (Salamanca), 1 km von
der Hauptstadt; Stierkampfschule - plaza de
tientas.

6. TURISMO

6.1. EXCURSIONES DESDE SALAMANCA A
LA PROVINCIA
EXCURSIONS DE SALAMANQUE A LA
PROVINCE
EXCURSIONS FROM SALAMANCA TO
THE PROVINCE
AUSFLÜGE VON SALAMANCA IN DIE
PROVINZ

I. Ruta Teresiana
I. Route de Ste. Thérèse
I. Santa Teresas'route
I. Route der Heiligen Therese

Salamanca, Alba de Tormes, Santiago de la
Puebla, Macotera, Peñaranda de Bracamonte, Salamanca (107 kilómetros).
ALBA DE TORMES. Convento de M. M. Carmelitas, fundado por Santa Teresa, donde se
guardan sus restos. Torreón del castillo, residencia ducal de Alba.

SANTIAGO DE LA PUEBLA Y MACOTERA. Interesantes iglesias de estilo isabelino.

Salamanque, Alba de Tormes, Santiago de la
Puebla, Macotera, Peñaranda de Braca-
monte, Salamanque (107 Km.).

ALBA DE TORMES. Couvent des Carmélites
fondé par Ste. Thérèse et où elle est enterrée.
Donjon du château, residence des ducs
d'Albe.

SANTIAGO DE LA PUEBLA ET MACOTERA. In-
téressantes églises de style isabellien.

Salamanca, Alba de Tormes, Santiago de la
Puebla, Macotera, Peñaranda de Bracamonte, Salamanca (107 kms.).

ALBA DE TORMES. Convent of the Carmelites, founded by St. Teresa, where her remains are buried, Torreón del Castillo. Residence of the Dukes of Alba.

SANTIAGO DE LA PUEBLA AND MACOTERA. Interesting churches in Isabelline style.

Salamanca, Alba de Tormes, Santiago de la Puebla, Macotera, Peñaranda de Bracamonte, Salamanca (107 km.).
ALBA DE TORMES. Von der Heiligen Therese gegr. Karmeliterinnen-Kloster, in dem ihre sterblichen Überreste aufbewahrt werden. Festungsturm des Schlosses, Wohnsitz der Herzöge von Alba.
SANTIAGO DE LA PUEBLA Y MACOTERA. Interessante Kirchen im isabellinischen Stil.

II. **Ruta de la sierra**
II. **Route de la montagne**
II. **Mountain route**
II. **Gebirgsroute**

Salamanca, Puente del Congosto, Candelario, Béjar, Miranda del Castañar, Sequeros, Mogarraz, La Alberca, Portillo de las Batuecas. La Peña de Francia, Tamames, Salamanca (267 kilómetros).
Típicos pueblos serranos, destacando La Alberca (monumento nacional), castillos en Puente del Congosto y Miranda del Castañar. Santuario en la Peña de Francia.

Salamanque, Puente del Congosto, Candelario, Béjar, Miranda del Castañar, Sequeros, Mogarraz, La Alberca, Portillo de las Batuecas, La Peña de Francia, Tamames, Salamanque (267 Km.).
Villages typiques de la montagne, dont La Alberca est le plus intéressant (monument national); châteaux à Puente del Congosto, Miranda del Castañar. Sanctuaire à la Peña de Francia.

Salamanca, Puente del Congosto, Candelario, Béjar, Miranda del Castañar, Sequeros, Mogarraz, La Alberca. Portillo de las Batuecas, La Peña de Francia, Tamames, Salamanca (267 kms).
Typical mountain villages, specially La Alberca (national monument), castles at Puente del Congosto and Miranda del Castañar. Sanctuary at Peña de Francia.

Salamanca, Puente del Congosto, Candelario, Béjar, Miranda del Castañar, Sequeros, Mogarraz, La Alberca, Portillo de las Batuecas, La Peña de Francia, Tamames, Salamanca (267 km).
Typische Gebirgsdörfer, von denen La Alberca (Nationaldenkmal) hervorsticht, Schlösser in Puente del Congosto und Miranda del Castañar. Heiligtum in la Peña de Francia.

III. **Ruta de Ciudad Rodrigo**
III. **Route de Ciudad Rodrigo**
III. **Ciudad Rodrigo route**
III. **Route Ciudad Rodrigo**

Salamanca, Ciudad Rodrigo, Salamanca (178 kilómetros).
CIUDAD RODRIGO. Núcleo fortificado, monumentos románicos y góticos. Destacan la Catedral, el Castillo de Enrique II (hoy Parador de Turismo), varios palacios y casas señoriales.

Salamanque, Ciudad Rodrigo, Salamanque (178 Km.).
CIUDAD RODRIGO. Ville forteresse, monuments romans et gothiques. Voir surtout la Cathédrale, le Château d'Henri II (transformé aujourd'hui en Parador Touristique) et plusieurs palais et demeures seigneuriales.

Salamanca, Ciudad Rodrigo, Salamanca (178 kms).
CIUDAD RODRIGO: fortified center with Roman and Gothic monuments. The Cathedral, the castle of Henry II (today «Parador» for Tourists) and other palaces and residential houses are of special interest.

Salamanca, Ciudad Rodrigo, Salamanca (178 km).
CIUDAD RODRIGO. Festungszentrum, romanische und gotische Monumente. Die Kathedrale, das Schloss von Enrique II. (staatl. Touristenhotel) und mehrere Paläste und herrschaftliche Häuser treten besonders hervor.

IV. **Ruta de los Arribes del Duero y los Pantanos**
IV. **Route du haut Douro («arribes») et des reservoirs**
IV. **Route along the shores of the river Duero and reservoirs**
IV. **Route los Arribes del Duero und Talsperren**

Salamanca, Ledesma, Vitigudino, Salto de Aldeadávila, Salto de Saucelle, La Fregeneda, Lumbrales, San Felices de los Gallegos, Vitigudino, Salamanca (274 kilómetros).
La zona de los «arribes del Duero» es de gran belleza paisajística entre berrocales y peñascos. El Salto de Aldeadávila es el más alto de Europa. En San Felices de los Gallegos, murallas y Torre del Homenaje.

Salamanque, Ledesma, Vitigudino, Salto de Aldeadávila, Salto de Saucelle, La Fregeneda, Lumbrales, San Felices de los Gallegos, Vitigudino, Salamanque (274 Km.).
La zone des «arribes» du Douro a un très beau paysage, entre ses rochers granitiques et ses rocailles. La chute d'eau d'Aldeadávila est la plus haute d'Europa. A San Felices de los Gallegos, murailles et Tour de l'Hommage.

Salamanca, Ledesma, Vitigudino, Salto (Dam) de Aldeadávila, Salto de Saucelle, La Fregeneda, Lumbrales, San Felices de los Gallegos, Vitigudino, Salamanca (274 kms).

The district of the «arribes» (shores) of the Duero has a very beautiful landscape between rocks and mountains. The Aldeadávila Dam is the highest in Europe. In San Felices de los Gallegos, there are city walls and Torre del Homenaje.

Salamanca, Ledesma, Vitigudino, Wasserfall von Aldeadávila, Wasserfall von Saucelle, La Fregeneda, Lumbrales, San Felices de los Gallegos, Vitigudino, Salamanca (274 km.).
Das Gebiet «Los arribes» del Duero bietet mit seiner felsigen Landschaft eine besondere Schönheit. Der Wasserfall von Aldeadávila ist der höchste Europas. In San Felices de los Gallegos Mauern und Ehrenturm.

V. **Ruta del toro bravo**
V. **Route du taureau de course**
V. **Brave bull's route**
V. **Route des toro bravo (windel Stieres)**

Salamanca, Robliza de Cojos, Matilla de los Caños, Vecinos, Salamanca (69 kilómetros). Interesante paisaje; bella estampa del ganado bravo en pleno campo charro.

Salamanque, Robliza de Cojos, Matilla de los Caños, Vecinos, Salamanque (69 Km).
Paysage intéressant; magnifique tableau de taureaux de course en pleine campagne de Salamanque.

Salamanca, Robiza de Cojos, Matilla de los Caños, Vecinos, Salamanca (69 kms).
Interesting landscape, a wonderful display of the bulls, on Salamanca land.

Salamanca, Robliza de Cojos, Matilla de los Caños, Vecinos, Salamanca (69 km).
Interessante Landschaft; schönes Bild mit Stierherden im «campo charro».

6.2. **OTROS LUGARES DE INTERES**
AUTRES SITES D'INTERET
OTHER PLACES OF INTEREST
ANDERE INTERESSANTE ORTE

BALNEARIO DE LEDESMA. A 28 kilómetros de la capital. Tratamiento del reumatismo, neuralgias, ciática, enfermedades de la piel, bronquitis, catarros, etc. Hotel del Balneario, de 2.ª categoría.

BALNEAIRE DE LEDESMA. A 28 Km. de la capital. Traitement du rhumatisme, de la néuralgie, sciatique, maladies de la peau, bronchites, catarrhes, etc. Hôtel Balnéaire, 2ème catégorie.

LEDESMA SPA. 28 kms from the capital. Treatment for rheumatism, neuralgias, sciatica, skin, diseases, bronchitis, colds, etc. Spa Hotel, 2nd category.

BADE- UND KURORT LEDESMA. 28 km von der Stadt entfernt. Rheumatismus, Neuralgien, Hüftweh, Hautkrankheiten, Bronchitis, Katarrhe usw. Kurhotel 2. Kategorie.

BALNEARIO DE RETORTILLO. A 72 kilómetros de la capital. Tratamiento del reumatismo, cardiopatías reumáticas compensadas, bronquitis, catarros, dermatitis secas, etcétera. Hotel del Balneario, de 2.ª categoría y Pensión del Balneario, también de 2.ª.

BALNEAIRE DE RETORTILLO. A 72 Km. de la capitale. Traitement du rhumatisme, de la cardiopathie rhumatisme compensé, bronchites, dermatites sèches, etc. Hôtel Balnéaire, 2ème catégorie et Pension Balnéaire, également de 2ème catégorie.

RETORTILLO SPA. 72 kms. from the capital. Treatment of rheumatism, rheumatic cardiovascular disorders, bronchitis, colds, dry dermatitis, etc. Spa Hotel 2nd category and Boarding House, also second category.

BADE- UND KURORT RETORTILLO. 72 km von der Stadt entfernt. Rheumatismus, rheumatische Herzleiden Bronchitis, Katarrhe trockene Hautentzündungen usw. Kurhotel 2. Kategorie; Kurpension ebenfalls 2. Kategorie.

6.3. **RUTAS INTERPROVINCIALES**
ITINERAIRES INTERPROVINCIAUX
INTERPROVINCIAL ROUTES
STRASSEN INNERHALB DER PROVINZEN

Ruta de la Lusitania española
Itinéraire de la Lusitanie espagnole
The Spanish Lusitanian Road
Route der spanischen Lusitania

Salamanca, Cáparra, Alcántara, Alconetar, Cáceres, Mérida y regreso (680 Km.).

Salamanque, Cáparra, Alcántara, Alconetar, Cáceres, Mérida et retour (680 km).

Salamanca, Cáparra, Alcántara, Alconetar, Cáceres, Mérida and back (680 km).

Salamanca, Cáparra, Alcántara, Alconetar, Cáceres, Mérida und zurück (680 km).

Ruta del románico leonés
Itinéraire du Roman Léonais
The romanic Road of Leon
Route des romanischen León

Salamanca, Tordesillas, Toro, Palencia, Frómista, Villasirga, Carrión, Sahagún, León, Benavente, Zamora, Salamanca (587 Km.).

Salamanque, Tordesillas, Toro, Palence, Frómista, Villasirga, Carrión, Sahagún, León,
Benavente, Zamora, Salamanque (587 km).

Salamanca, Tordesillas, Toro, Palencia, Frómista, Villasirga, Carrión, Sahagún, León,
Benavente, Zamora, Salamanca (587 km).

*Salamanca, Tordesillas, Toro, Palencia, Fró-
mista, Villasirga, Carrión, Sahagún, León,
Benavente, Zamora, Salamanca (587 km).*

Ruta de los santuarios
Itinéraire des sanctuaires
The Sanctuaires Road
Route der Heiligtümer

Salamanca, Alba de Tormes, Segovia, Fuen-
cisla, Avila, Béjar, Peña de Francia, Guada-
lupe y regreso (305 Km.).

*Salamanque, Alba de Tormes, Ségovie, Fuen-
cisla, Avila, Béjar, Peña de Francia, Guada-
lupe et retour. (305 km).*

Salamanca, Alba de Tormes, Segovia, Fuen-
cisla, Avila, Béjar, Peña de Francia, Guada-
lupe and back (305 km).

*Salamanca, Alba de Tormes, Segovia, Fuen-
cisla, Avila, Béjar, Peña de Francia, Guada-
lupe und zurück (305 km).*

Ruta mudéjar
Itinéraire «mudéjar»
The Mohammedan Road
Mudéjar-Route

Salamanca, Peñaranda, Madrigal, Arévalo,
Coca, Medina del Campo, Tordesilla y regreso (305 Km.).

*Salamanque, Peñaranda, Madrigal, Arévalo,
Coca, Medina del Campo, Tordesillas, et retour
(305 km).*

Salamanca, Peñaranda, Madrigal, Arévalo,
Coca, Medina del Campo, Tordesillas and
back (305 km).

*Salamanca, Peñaranda, Madrigal, Arévalo,
Coca, Medina del Campo, Tordesillas und zurück (305 km).*

Ruta de los embalses del Duero
Itinéraire des barrages du Douro
The Road through the lakes of Duero
Route der Duero-Stauseen

Salamanca, Saucelle, Aldeadávila, Villarino,
Fermoselle, Villalcampo, Ricobayo, Zamora,
Salamanca (385 Km.).

*Salamanque, Saucelle, Aldeadávila, Villarino,
Fermoselle, Ricobayo, Zamora, Salamanque
(385 km).*

Salamanca, Saucelle, Aldeadávila, Villarino,
Fermoselle, Villalcampo, Ricobayo, Zamora,
Salamanca (385 km).

*Salamanca, Saucelle, Aldeadávila, Villarino,
Fermoselle, Villalcampo, Ricobayo, Zamora,
Salamanca (385 km).*

Ruta de la Plata
Itinéraire de l'argent
The Silverway
Route «de la Plata»

Carretera N-630. Gijón, Oviedo, León, Benavente, Zamora, Salamanca, Béjar, Plasencia,
Cáceres, Mérida, Zafra, Sevilla o viceversa
(720 Km., una dirección sola).

*Route Nationale n.° 630. Gijón, Oviedo, León,
Benavente, Zamora, Salamanque, Béjar, Plasencia, Cáceres, Mérida, Zafra, Séville ou
vice-versa (720 km dans un seule direction).*

Highway N.°-630. Gijón, Oviedo, León, Benavente, Zamora, Salamanca, Béjar, Plasencia,
Cáceres, Mérida, Zafra, Sevilla or viceversa
(720 km, just one direction).

*Carretera N-630. Gijón, Oviedo, León, Bena-
vente, Zamora, Salamanca, Béjar, Plasencia,
Cáceres, Mérida, Zafra, Sevilla oder umge-
kehrt (720 km, nur in einer Richtung).*

**6.4. DISTANCIAS KILOMETRICAS DESDE
SALAMANCA
DISTANCES KILOMETRIQUES DE SA-
LAMANCA
DISTANCES IN KILOMETERS FROM SA-
LAMANCA
ENTFERNUNGEN IN KM. SALAMANCA
NACH:**

Alba de Tormes 18
Béjar 70
Ciudad Rodrigo 88
Ledesma 34
Peñaranda de Bracamonte 41
Sequeros 94
Vitigudino 68
Fuentes de Oñoro (Portugal) 117

• • •

Avila 97
Cáceres 211
Madrid 212
Portugal (Guarda) 166
Zamora 62

25

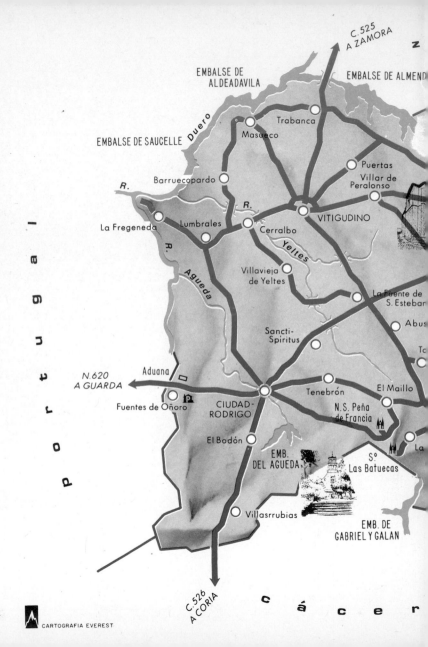